AN ELEPHANT IN THE LOBBY

Scenes from a North-east Scotland childhood

Douglas Willis

To Alasdair and Catriona

Other books by Douglas Willis:

Sand and Silence (University of Aberdeen)

Discovering the Black Isle (John Donald)

A Scottish Nature Diary (John Donald)

The Story of Crofting in Scotland (John Donald)

Crofting (John Donald)

Copyright 2012

Douglas Willis

ISBN: 978-1-905787-35-7

Printed by

FOR THE RIGHT REASONS

Printer & Publisher

60 Grant Street, Inverness, IV3 8BS

fortherightreasons@rocketmail.com

Tel:01463 718844 or 07717457247

CONTENTS

Chapter 1: The way it was ....

At the time I'm writing about here, the war hadn't long ended and things were settling back to normality in the close-knit community into which I was born. In our quiet corner of North-east Scotland, stirrings of change were in the air but the basic pattern of daily living was much as it had been for generations. The men of the Gordon Highlanders, who had left their jobs in our small market town and the surrounding area to take up arms for king and country, had settled back into the same routines as before. Those who didn't come home had their names added to the grey granite war memorial. On a brighter note, that symbol of scarcity and austerity, the Government ration book, was finding less and less use. There was a palpable feeling of optimism in the air; a sense of expectation that better days must surely be round the corner.

The house in which I lived until the age of ten was rented, rundown and much in need of renovation but it was a homely place in which to grow, and the memory of the days I spent there has remained satisfyingly undimmed. It stood where the town abruptly ended and the spreading green acres of the wide howe, with their criss-crossing drysteen dykes, stretched out beyond. In truth, both in character and in function, the place had more the feel of country village. There was no outward sprawl of new house building to blur the divide between town and countryside as tends to be the way of things today. The one depended on the other; existing in the landscape in a time honoured sort of social symbiosis. The location of our house was to have a profound influence on my later life, for it was in the surrounding country places that my eyes were opened to the fascination of the natural world.

In the prescribed landscape of this place of my early upbringing, the distant dark hill of Bennachie was an ever present reference point, a familiar friend casting a benign eye over the surrounding farmlands and imparting a sense of place to all who lived within sight of it. As hills and mountains go, this was no Ben Nevis. Yet, to the eye of a child, there was a suggestion of the volcanic about the way the dark massif rose steeply to its Mither Tap summit, especially if a puff of white cloud should happen to be passing above. Such was its drawing power that now, after decades in exile, I can shut my eyes and effortlessly conjure up the hill's distinctive outline.

I was raised by my great granny who had already lived out her three score years and ten (and another few years besides) before I ever made an entry into this world, so there were bound to be elements of the old fashioned in the way life was lived at home. In so many ways she belonged to an earlier age. She was my mentor in Doric, the rich and colourful, down to earth spik of the North-east that was my first language. Such things form an invisible thread in your life when you're very young, but I came in time to recognise how my granny had instilled in me the values that shaped her own life. In memory, I see her now: silver-haired and clad in her usual wrap-over pinny, invariably black or grey with an all-over, unostentatious pattern of tiny red or white flowers. When one wore out, a replacement was obtained from the drapery department within the Northern Co-operative Society's grand Victorian arcade in Loch Street in Aberdeen on one of her rare sallies, dressed in black coat and hat, into the Toon on an Alexander's Bluebird bus to collect her Co-op dividend. She would have considered making her purchases nowhere else but from a shop belonging to the Co-op. The Society's dividend ("Co-opie divvie", she called it) was a key part of her home financial management; the past term's purchasing loyalty duly rewarded when the Society declared its dividend to its customers who were also its shareholders. The long hair was pulled severely back into a bun and secured by a fearsomely long pin. This, together with the well-lined face, gave her a stern kind of look that belied a warm and loving nature and a generosity that was extended beyond the bounds of her own family to anyone who was in need. In our house, sharing was an everyday part of life; spontaneous and generous in its nature.

There's a thing called the slow food movement these days that extols the virtue of an unhurried approach to preparation and appreciation. Looking back on it now, I think there was something akin to that for youngsters in the time and place I'm talking about here. We seemed to be allowed to develop at a more leisurely pace, growing in an unhurried, flavoursome way with none of the pressures to grow up quickly that are placed upon the modern generation. In so many ways, the scenes that follow are from a different age: a time when my granny and I sat at home at night in the pallid glow of the hissing gas light with no television for distraction; when the coalman's horse was a familiar friend, and when we knew the names of the birds and other creatures that inhabited the country places on our doorstep. Our developing lives were enriched by the colourful characters we encountered and, in the matter of play, few things came our way that had been manufactured or bought. 'Second hand' was a familiar phrase and an essential concept in home economics. Whoever said that recycling is a modern idea never existed in the days when hand-me-down clothes were a key element in living, the garments passed down through a family, or from family to family, till they finally wore out.

I was fortunate in having pals of the same age who lived close by. They make an occasional appearance as Ian and Geordie in the pages that follow. The former, more reserved and with lank black hair trimmed unflatteringly in one of his mother's kitchen bowl-cuts, was taller and skinnier and showing the signs of turning into a gangly sort of youth. By contrast, the latter was the podgy one; red-haired, freckle-faced, and ever on the lookout for an opportunity for devilment. I ought to complete things with a picture of the third of the trio but I'm not sure how I should describe myself at the time. There was no camera about the house, so I have few images from that age. In build, I suppose I was in between the two others but such photos as do exist show my most noteworthy feature to be the head of curly fair hair. This could be a real pain in the neck when some old wifie would run her hand across it and make remarks about its appearance; remarks which she no doubt thought were complimentary but which I certainly didn't take as any compliment. But the seasons of life have moved on and I'd be glad of such a thick warming cover these days when the chill winds of autumn blow over a now sadly incomplete thatch.

With the ill-matched duo, I shared the walk to and from school. In summer we enjoyed forays into the countryside, especially on the weeks when we were released from the foostie confines of our classroom; days that were satisfyingly long, as the summer days of memory invariably seem to be. The three of us made the daily trek of the better part of a mile to our community's austere Victorian tribute to established education, in which our teacher managed the class with a firm hand, as tended to be the way of the time. The philosophy of the age was that the path through school life should be laced with strictness, and the education we received was sound. What I write about classroom life, I write in the knowledge that it can cause no offence to the living. In fact, we all thought the teachers in school must be aged about ninety. But pupils have always had a tendency to regard their teachers as old. I think I went through all my school days, primary and secondary, without encountering a single one that seemed in any way young. Perhaps their chosen profession had aged them prematurely.

There is no sequential time flow in the writing that follows, rather a random setting down of scenes and incidents from home, school and countryside. It was born out of a desire to pass on something about my early days to my two children, whose growing took place in very different times and circumstances.

Chapter 2: The coalman's horse

The coalman's horse was much beset by flatulence. Had it been living in today's world, it might have been classed as a major source of greenhouse gas emission for it seemed to be permanently afflicted by loudly trumpeted emissions of wind strong enough to register on the Beaufort Scale. Small boys have always taken a keen interest in such matters and, needless to say, as Geordie, Ian and I swung our schoolbags at one another and generally capered about on the way home from school, we always kept an eye open for the friendly brown Clydesdale that dutifully pulled his load of blackened hessian sacks of Shilbottle, Welsh, dross, and suchlike varieties of coal around the doors. The equally blackened coalman meanwhile advertised his presence outside the houses with his own distinctive street cry: a repeated and prolonged shout of "CO--**AL!**"

Jock, for so the beast was called, would meanwhile shake his head with attached moo bag to reach the last of the oats with his long pink and grey tongue. Jock's moo bag was a worn and faded green canvas container attached over his mouth and replenished from time to time with a handful of oats to keep him happy while his boss delivered the sacks on his back and disappeared round behind the houses to folk's coal sheds. Once he'd retrieved the last of his treat, however, he became like a thrawn bairn, impatiently throwing back his head, rattling his harness and wanting to move the cart on towards the next house when he knew he wasn't supposed to. As far as the three of us were concerned, any encounter with the horse was a guarantee of entertainment. Naturally, we took a considerable interest in such an entertaining beast and Jock always seemed pleased when we stopped to clap his dusty head. When this was rewarded with a flatuous fanfare, as happened with regularity, we naturally fell about laughing. "Ye'd hear yon horse a mile awa," asserted Geordie. "The coal mannie widna need tae shout tae let fowk ken he wis comin. A'body wad ken fine wi that horse aboot the place." At this he produced a rude and resounding raspberry which made us laugh all the more.

From time to time, Jock would lift his tail and deposit a heap of manure on to the road. This gift excited interest on two fronts. Keen gardeners would arrive on the scene, shovel in hand, ready to remove the free fertilizer for their roses. Deposits left outside non-gardening households attracted the attention of the local spurgies who regarded the malodorous heaps as manna from heaven, spending hours diligently pecking over them in search of grains that had passed intact through Jock's defective digestive tract. Without a doubt, Jock was one of the characters of the place; a windy wonder who supplied endless entertainment to us loons, as well as being a benefactor of local gardeners and sparrows.

An incident occurred concerning our good friend the horse that kept us amused for months afterwards, even at the mere thought of it. On our way home from school one afternoon, we were taking turns at kicking a fallen lump of coal along the gutter when we came upon the familiar form of Jock, idly passing the time between the cart shafts while he waited for the coalman to reappear from behind a house. We were as familiar as Jock was with the coalman's word of command to move on: a double click of the tongue which only Geordie could manage to imitate in a really authentic way. And, what's more, only he had the nerve to try it out; the other two of us would never have dared. As Geordie got his tongue into the required position and made the double click of command, Jock's ears cocked up and off he dutifully moved with cart and coal on to the next house. We were much impressed, though wary that Jock's master might appear at any moment and jalouse what had happened. With the coalman still not appearing (doubtless detained by a haranguing from some wifie about the poor burning quality of the coal), and getting carried away with his success, Geordie boldly repeated the command. At this, Jock turned his head round and gave a look as much as to say that he was more than happy to continue with the prank, so off he set again, dozens of hundredweight sacks of coal on board, stopping outside the house of the next customer. This second time was a bit of a step too far and the three of us began to take cold feet, so off we fled up the road, dodging into a lane to peep out and view the proceedings from a distance. We hadn't long to wait for the coalman to emerge. At first he didn't even notice Jock's disappearance, as his head was down while he fumbled about among the coins inside the big brown leather money bag slung round his neck. When he realised that Jock was now some distance along the road, he was livid and we could hear him roar "Jock, ye auld b*****! Fit the hell are ye playin at?" As we teeted round the corner, we could see him catch up with the horse and attempt the awkward task of reversing the cart to where it should properly have been, a manoeuvre in which Jock was evidently none too keen to participate. We never dared try the trick again. The coalman seemed to have no inkling of the part we played in the curious case of the disappearing coal cart but I'll swear Jock never forgot that day as his ears always seemed to prick up whenever we passed him on the road. It was a sad day when Jock and his like vanished off the streets and were replaced by motor lorries producing exhaust products of a type of no value whatsoever to either gardeners or spurgies.

The baker had already proceeded down the road of motorisation. His brown van had a bit of roof that slid out behind as a shelter for himself and the unwrapped bread and rolls carefully arranged in rows in shallow wooden trays. At each stop he blew a shrill whistle and the long trays were drawn out for customer inspection, releasing delicious wafts of new bread smell. Plain items, such as butteries, softies and flat girdle scones were arranged in one tray, while what were termed funcies, fancy cakes with garish pink and yellow icings, reposed in another. Some of the latter had tiny silver boolies on top and contained a sickly sweet fondant filling. The cakes we called flee cemeteries had so many black currants packed between their pastry layers that they certainly did resemble a mass fly burial. I didn't care for these but did like sair heedies which were round sponge cakes with a bit of thin greaseproof paper wrapped round the side with the baker's name printed on it and big bits of sugar on top that I liked to eat off first. They bore some resemblance to a bandaged head, hence their name. Bread was known always to us as loaf. It came in a variety of shapes, from the smooth pan variety, with its weight shown in relief along its side off the baking tin, to the ill-shaped plain version with crusts tough enough to test the strongest teeth. Sliced bread was entirely unheard of in our household. Some folk dipped the crusts in their tea to relieve themselves of the effort of trying to chew the un-chewable. This approach was much favoured by old people who either had no teeth left or hadn't bothered putting their false ones in. Crusts were never rejected in our house and any bread that was less than fresh was made into a bread pudding with a few currants on top or eaten, along with warm milk and a sprinkling of sugar, as saps.

Although carts and vans brought coal, bread, milk and fish to the door, ours was a market town and so we were well supplied by a range of shops that served the surrounding rural area as well as the local populace. Of these, the saddler's was the most intriguing: a dark Aladdin's cave filled with hanging bits and pieces and smelling strongly of new leather. The demand for repairs to saddles, harnesses, canvas belts for threshing mills, horses' moo bags and the like was on the wane since working horses were in steep decline, but he could turn his hand to mending items as diverse as ladies' leather handbags and hand-me-down schoolbags where the stitching had come undone. He was also a purveyor of raffia which looked like long strands of pale dry grass but actually came from a faraway palm. It was in demand for crafts in and out of school. Strands dyed in different colours hung from hooks on the wall. A variation of the same smell hung about the souter's shop, but this time it was a mix of new leather and shoe polish. His skills were directed towards keeping footwear fit for purpose, applying new leather soles, heels, segs and tackets as necessary to keep them roadworthy and put off the evil hour of having to shell out for a new pair.

The droggist was what we called the chemist. His premises were distinguished by a big gold mortar and pestle fixed above the door, as well as the elegant glass jars of intriguing coloured liquids lined up in the two windows. What was in them I'm not quite sure but they certainly made eye-catching window adornments. The droggist himself, a serious man in a white coat, stood in front of rows of mysterious dark brown wooden drawers with queer-like names in gold lettering on the front that didn't seem to make any sense. From here, out of large containers, he dispensed creams and ointments for the afflicted into circular, waxed card boxes. A hard-covered notebook, ominously marked POISON REGISTER, reposed on the counter and had to be signed by anybody wanting to obtain such things as methylated spirits. It was here that my granny obtained the supply of liquid paraffin that she regarded as a requisite for a regular, healthy life.

Most everyday household needs were obtained from the general merchants who lived up to their name by stocking a wide variety of goods, ranging from food and firelighters to mothballs and mouse traps. Packaging wasn't what it is today and things tended to be stored in close proximity, so it came as no surprise if you thought there might be a hint of paraffin flavour to the butter you'd just spread across your oatcake. Plastic carrier bags were as yet unheard of and straw or wicker baskets were much in vogue for carrying home the eerans. Whenever I was sent to the Co-opie for sugar I enjoyed seeing the grocer lift it out with a rounded metal scoop from a thick brown hessian sack and carefully weigh it out on a set of brass scales on the long wooden counter. There was a strange word printed on the side of the sacks and I always thought what a grand sounding thing that might be. It was a considerable disappointment to discover later that 'granulated' simply meant that the sugar was in grains, which seems to me to be stating the obvious. The grocer, in his brown overall, tipped the sugar from the shiny brass pan on his scales into a brown paper pyock. This was then carefully secured at the top with a length of fine white twine pulled from a metal dispenser with a built-in cutter that sat permanently on the counter.

Things didn't happen quickly in the shop but that was the way of things and you just got used to it. It gave the customers (and the shopkeeper himself, it goes without saying) a chance to catch up on any gossip with a view to passing it on at a later time. When I was sent to get some syrup, I had to bring an empty jam jar, watching as the sticky golden material flowed viscously out of the tap at the bottom of a drum. Commodities often arrived in bulk in wooden boxes and were then cut up or poured according to the customer's needs. The Commonwealth played a major part in furnishing the nation with its food supply. Slabs of red, tongue-nipping, extra mature Canadian cheddar cheese were cut off with a bit of thin wire. Even butter from faraway New Zealand, which some folk believed was golden yellow because their dairy cows lived in a sunnier clime than ours, came in bulk and was scooped on to a sheet of greaseproof paper. Wrappings were simple in the extreme. There was no wasteful packaging;

the throwaway society had yet to evolve. Life was less hurried and the shops were where snippets of general interest were exchanged and scandals spoken about in hushed tones. It was here that the world was set to rights, and in that sense the shop queues fulfilled an important social role.

Living so close to the countryside brought lots of benefits, not least the fact that I had a foot in another world, that of the nearby small farms. I enjoyed the times when I had contact with these places, seeing the resident cocks with their sickle-shaped tails proclaim their lordship from the top of steaming midden heaps, with a loud and throaty cock-a-doodle-doo, and watching as the soft-eyed house cows were hand-milked in the byre. At harvest time, when the big orange disc of a hairst meen rose above the horizon in the early evening, the binders, still sometimes horse-drawn, worked on till dusk, cutting the ripe corn and dropping the bound sheaves as they passed. The harvest squad, augmented by a neighbour or two, followed on behind, arranging the sheaves into upright stooks that let the wind pass through so that they could dry before being gathered into the stack-yard.

At a later date, it was time for the sheaves, which had been carefully stacked by the men into tight circular rucks in the farm yard, to be taken down again when the threshing mill, or, as we said, the thrashin mull, arrived. This travelling mill was a sight to behold: a pink-painted wooden monster of a thing on metal-rimmed wheels that was trailed slowly from farm to farm in the district, consuming each precious crop of oats and spitting out the grain from the chaff. When the mill started up with a shuddering noise and a moving canvas belt, it was time for the men to start the task of feeding the sheaves into the beast's insatiable jaws. In no time, a rhythm of forking was established against the background whirr of the machine, and the pale, light chaff was soon parting company with the heavier grains.

The day of the threshing was a fascination to any child for the colour, sounds and drama that went with it, and none of us would have missed it for the world. As time passed, wild scenes were enacted as the rucks came down and fewer and fewer of the sheaves remained. Those that were left had become a last refuge for the battalions of rats and mice which had taken up a dry and comfortable existence inside. As their cosy world collapsed about their ears, they had to flee the warm sanctuary they'd enjoyed for weeks on full board, scattering in all directions, accompanied by yelps and squeals from the ragbag pack of dogs that had come to have a good time chasing after the panicking creatures as they raced out. It was a day when the men worked till the sweat stood out on their foreheads and the womenfolk kept them fuelled with scones fresh off the girdle, along with hot, sweet tea from huge brown enamel kettles. The whole process was as much entertainment as essential task and the presence of the three of us was tholed as long as we kept at a distance from the machinery with its potentially dangerous moving parts. It was as good a show as we enjoyed at the circus and we cheered the rodent exodus and the ensuing chase, hoping that a big scary rat with its long scaly tail wouldn't escape the attention of the dogs and head in our direction. The men made nicky-tams of their wide trouser legs by tying a length of binder tow below their knees to heist up the legs of their dungarees and stop the bottoms trailing in the dirt. But we thought it might be to deter any fleeing young rat or moosie from running up a trouser leg and seeking refuge in a place where you'd much rather they didn't go, and so we stood and watched with eagle-eyed vigilance in case some fugitive rodent might make a dash for safety up the leg of our short breeks.

Chapter 3: An elephant in the lobby

I grew up knowing the scary sounds of the African night. If that should sound at odds with what's gone before, I should maybe bring things down to earth straight away by explaining that our house lay close to an open area of ground where travelling circuses set up their big tops - or not so big tops, depending on the scale of the outfit. There was no shortage of small circuses on the road and we could generally look forward to one putting in an appearance each summer. When the lions started roaring into the night from their cramped travelling cages, it sounded as if they were just outside. When I went to bed and shut my eyes, I could easily imagine I was in the darkest bit of darkest Africa and kept thinking that somebody my size would make a handy snack for a hungry lion on the prowl. At every resounding roar, I withdrew deeper under the thick woollen blankets, even though I knew that the ferocious sounding beasts must be firmly under lock and key – or rather I hoped they were, since they were so close to the house. The worrying thing was that, in class, our teacher had told us all about David Livingstone's exploits in Africa – and we all knew what happened to him when a lion got its sharp clooks in through his cotton sark.

There was a bit of a buzz about town in the days before a circus was due. Long before the brightly-painted white, red and yellow cavalcade of lorries, trailers and caravans arrived, its coming was the talk of the playground. Colourful advertising posters added a splash of the exotic to everyday window displays with their arrays of scrubbing brushes, pails and packets of Oxydol washing powder and the like. Others were pinned round well-creosoted telegraph poles. Some showed a picture of snarling lions with huge manes, and fangs so long that the artist who'd been commissioned to draw the beasts had obviously been told not to stint on the scary. The posters promised all manner of funny- and sad-faced clowns, not to mention daring trapeze artists, but my eye always scanned to see what sort of animals there might be a chance of seeing, whether it was lions, leopards or llamas. The idea of some of these creatures being trailed around from town to town on interminable public show fills me with distaste now, but for a child with a passion for wildlife it couldn't have been more exciting.

When the circus did at last hit town, the advertising machine was notched up a gear. The publicity van with its crackly black loudspeaker on the roof toured the streets broadcasting times of performances. Some circuses mounted a bit of a parade, with the most biddable of the livestock walking alongside clowns in colourful outfits and glamorous lady bareback riders in scanty costumes showing more exposed female flesh than the men of the place were generally used to. The most barefaced advertising stunt of all took place as we were leaving the school one afternoon when one of the circus men appeared at the gate with a tiny lion cub on a collar and lead. Naturally, we all clamoured around to pet the creature. Afterwards, we all went racing home to say that we'd been patting a **real** lion and could we please be allowed to go to the circus to see its father, perhaps (as I thought) the one on the poster with the massive mane and scary fangs.

From our house, we were well placed to view the steer-up when the battered old circus vehicles came spluttering in about, enveloped in choking clouds of blue exhaust. The arrival of the motley collection of lorries and trailers was quickly followed by the metallic ring of steel pegs being hammered into the ground as a squad of brawny circus hands heaved and hauled at the ropes to lift up the big canvas tent. When everything was in place, the tight cluster of brightly painted vehicles and trailers was an enticing world to any youngsters and Geordie, Ian and I couldn't have been better placed to make the most of it. We were naturally curious about the glamour world of the circus folk, but however amiable and charming the clowns might be in their baggy trousers, over-size shoes and painted faces during the shows, we soon discovered that they could be extremely disagreeable when they put their mind to it. One time, when we went wandering around their caravans, a clown with a mop of fake orange hair and a big red nose came out and told us, in language as colourful as his costume, to clear off - only that's not exactly the words he used.

Naturally, we were keen to see what was going on inside the mystery world of the big top outside performance times, when we could hear the crack of the ringmaster's whip and the voices of trainers shouting commands at their horses. There was only one way to get a look and that was to try to raise the bottom edge of the grass-stained white canvas and take a furtive peek inside. This was more easily said than done, however, and needed the combined efforts of the three of us to try to lift even a small section of the material. By lying down on the grass and peering in below the canvas we got a tantalising glimpse into an enticing world where bright arc lights shone down from supporting red poles above the ring and where the trapped air was heady with the smell of fresh horse dung and newly trampled grass. On one occasion, we hadn't lowered our voices enough and the next we knew was a shout from inside and the hard head of a brush being wielded with an accuracy that suggested it was no new experience having to dealing with nosey youngsters intent on getting a free look. Perhaps they wanted to protect not just the privacy of the entertainers but the whole mystique of the show. Maybe it was in the job description of the men who swept up the horse droppings to deal with tiresome wee loons as well. In which case, no wonder they were so grumpy; it was hardly the best combination. Anyway, the prospect of a wallop from a hard brush that had just been used to sweep up freshly produced horse manure was enough to make the three of us beat a hasty retreat. "Ah widna like tae get on the wrang side o thon chiel," I muttered as the three of us took off. "Aye," Ian agreed, "he'd a coorse kin o look aboot him."

Going to see the circus the legitimate, fee-paying way was a less hazardous experience. Interspersed with high-wire trapeze artists in their glittering, sequinned costumes, and clowns that were forever drenching one another with buckets of water, came the real nail biting stuff. Behind high metal bars, the lions snarled and pawed the air when their trainer advanced towards them, wooden stool in one hand and leather whip in the other. It was all heady stuff but for me it paled into insignificance compared to the chance to see the animals in close up. Admission to the menagerie incurred a small charge. It was open to the public at times when the animals weren't required for performing inside the big top. Within their own long tent, haughty looking liberty horses with sleek black or brown coats shared stalls with the odd zebra, llama or camel. With our teacher's passion for instilling general knowledge, I'd no problem remembering that "A one-humped camel is a dromedary; if two-humped, it's called a bactrian." One hump or two, I tended to give any camel I encountered a bit of a wide berth, as I'd been told that they'd perfected the art of spitting from a distance if they took an ill will at you.

Apart from the possibility of a bit of frothy camel spit landing about your person, health and safety, had it existed, would have had a field day at the very thought of somebody my size getting close up to a tetchy zebra since they're such strong animals, with the power to lash out with their back legs and inflict real injury. A line of trailers with vertical iron bars across their fronts housed the big cats, especially the lions which snarled at one another as they fought over the gory back end of a cow fetched in from the local knackery. "A pun o mince fae the butcher widna gyang far wi that ane" said an old mannie standing beside me, nodding at an impressive male lion that was making short work of a chunk of bloody raw meat. Sometimes the shows would also feature a tiger, which I really liked, or even a dark-coloured leopard with the menacing-sounding description of 'black panther' - and they could look **really** scary. The severely bored beasts padded back and fore in their cramped cells. Unkind though the lion taming performances may have been, I suppose they gave the incarcerated beasts a brief bit of exercise.

Some circuses were really small, with only one or two vans and caravans. They tended to feature what might be called a more economy range of livestock, specialising in things like dancing Shetland ponies and wee dogs dressed up in frilly frocks that jumped through fiery hoops and balanced shakily on two legs. They sometimes had a monkey on a lead that bared its teeth and pinched sweeties, making the adults burst into laughter and the kids into tears. What the constant diet of jube-jubes or pandrops did for the monkeys' insides is another matter. Sometimes these cash-strapped smaller outfits had to create their attractions on the cheap. One that I remember had a trailer made into a big cage filled with 'exotic' looking birds in every colour of the rainbow. But even I could see that the brightly plumaged birds sitting on the perches were no more than ordinary white doos that had been given a bit of treatment with the same kind of dye my granny occasionally used to change the colour of some garment.

But I've left the best till last. There was one circus with an amiable female elephant that was accompanied by an equally amiable, dark-skinned male attendant. The latter appeared in the performances dressed like an Indian maharajah, in a flowing red robe and matching silk turban with a huge sparkling diamond stuck on the front. More likely, it would have been a bit of polished glass reflecting in the big top lights but you don't think that way when you're little. During the day, he sometimes sat up on the elephant's back, using a long metal stick with a hooked end as he took her round and about for walks. The hook was a kind of substitute steering wheel, used to guide the beast by pulling on one or other of the flapping grey ears to indicate which direction he wanted her to take. On this occasion I noticed that the opportunist mahout had stopped beside some of the nearby houses to let the elephant take some slices of stale bread from the residents. Not only was this a shrewd marketing ploy, drumming up a bit of interest in the show, but it probably also saved on feeding bills. At any rate, the elephant seemed happy enough to take the bread, in spite of its dubious freshness, grasping piece after piece with the end of its trunk and passing them into its mouth.

Next day, seeing that the elephant was coming our way, I pleaded with my granny for a few bits of old loaf, and the two of us duly took up our position at the front door. According to plan, the attendant noticed the bread in my hand but his outsize charge was one step ahead of him and had already spied the food offering. Needless to say, the elephant needed no mahout's instruction to advance towards our front door. As she ambled forward, I was treated to a close-up of a surprisingly hairy mouth and two strangely small, quizzical dark eyes which fixed intently on me. I gulped and drew back. My courage suddenly deserted me and I withdrew further. Seeing the prospect of its food retreat out of range, the great beast advanced even more. This was the point at which disaster struck. In panic, I dropped the bread and fled to the back of the lobby. The elephant's wrinkly trunk came in the door, waving about in search of the promised treat. So near and yet so far, it must have been thinking, then the end began to twitch as its owner made a more determined effort to retrieve the fallen titbit. With her trunk already well into the lobby and her head pushed in firmly against the door jamb, the elephant began to shove even more, but still she couldn't reach. There was a certain inevitability to what happened next, this being the point at which the irresistible force began to have its inexorable way. The old, distempered lobby walls creaked and groaned and finally yielded to the strain caused by several tons of shoving elephant, before a white cloud of plaster descended over the brown linoleum. It was as though the house had been caught up in an earthquake. My granny, who was evidently a whole lot more at ease with pachyderms than I would ever have imagined, saved the day and further structural disaster by retrieving the bread and managing to throw it outside. Such was the extent of the elephant-inflicted damage that a neighbour had to be called in afterwards to re-plaster the whole area around the door. I certainly wasn't flavour of the month, but the most annoying thing was that the elephant, the cause of all the bother, had walked away scot free, with a complimentary snack into the bargain.

It was part of the attraction of the circus that it was here today and gone tomorrow. The departure of the show brought an end to days of colour and bustle and to nights that sounded as though we were living on the edge of a Tarzan film set. It was sad to see everything pack up and go but there was some compensation. Days of galloping horse hooves had imprinted a ring in the grass that we could use in our own make-believe circus play for weeks afterwards. A bit of string on the end of a stick made a reasonable imitation of a cracking whip and we could imagine the thrill of seeing the liberty horses nod their colourful head plumes as they performed to applause from the crowd seated on the tiered wooden benches. Best of all, we could gaze in awe at the enormous droppings left behind by the elephant after her diet of hay and stale loaf. In the following weeks we watched sadly as the khaki-coloured, pan loaf packages slowly disintegrated. It was Geordie who gave the last remnants a sad flick with a stick. "Weel, weel," he said with a wistful note to his voice, "that's the elephant dirt awa noo." There was no more to be said. Memories of the days the circus came to town slowly receded but each time I passed the fresh plaster I recalled with a cringe the day we had an elephant in the lobby.

Chapter 4: At the mart

If there was one day in the week that I really enjoyed it was mart day. Cattle have always been a key item of commerce in the North-east and when it came to the all important matter of buying and selling, every small market town used to have its livestock mart as a focus. From early morning on a mart day, a succession of cattle floats came trundling past our house, bringing in beasts from the country district round about and trailing in their wake a pungent smell that was a powerful mix of coo sharn and fumy exhaust. When they passed through the busy town centre, the wafting aroma gave the housewives who were unused to the smells of rural living a real scunner and made them wish they'd chosen a different time to go out and do their shopping.

Mart day brought a real stir to the place and involved more than just the buying and selling of stock. It was a day out for the fermin fowk and a boost for the local shopkeepers. At the same time, it was a weekly social gathering when wives took the chance to get a hurl in to town with their menfolk in order to attend to matters of a domestic nature. Of course, there were the travelling grocers' vans that made their way up the narrow roads with the basics. A barter system sometimes operated where fresh eggs from the hen house were traded with the van driver for household necessities. Other needs were met by the town shops which supplied items as varied as undergarments from the draper's glass-fronted wooden cabinets and flour and baking soda from the general merchants' well stocked shelves.

Mart day provided an opportunity for a good claik with likeminded womenfolk from round about, while the serious-faced men spent the day among the bustle of the mart itself, whether intent on transacting business or not. Just as the staff who worked at the mart had their 'uniform' of blue dungarees with the front bib fastened up with two silver clasps, and with heavy tackety beets on their feet, so the fermers came in to town in their standard garb of overcoats and checked cloth bonnets. It was a mark of the brotherhood of the land, perhaps, that they knew one another by the names of the places they worked, names which were often abbreviated from the full version. The incumbent of Mains of Muirden, for example, would be known to everybody round the district simply as 'Muiry.'

Pipe smoking was a feature of the age and many of the men had an addiction to the strongest tobaccos which they smoked in stubby old pipes. Out of little holes on the top of silver caps rose clouds of Bogie Roll reek. The source of the eye-watering fumes was the solid black twist of tobacco which they shaved with a pocket knife, the same implement that might have prised a stone out of a working horse's hoof earlier in the day or released the trapped air from the belly of a bloated yowe lying on her back in a park with her legs in the air. From time to time, they took a sideways spit before continuing with the business of keeping their pipes alight. I was mightily impressed by the way the pipe smokers could manage a good spit. Years of practice had raised it to something of an art form. After a good, throat-clearing haach, they never failed to summon up a good projectile and could send it unerringly in its intended direction. Had spitting featured in the Olympics, I reckon they'd have come away with a medal for it. In a house I went to occasionally, the old man was invariably to be found sitting in his easy chair at the fire. No matter how hot it was in the room, he still had on his bonnet and thick woollen jersey. Much to my delight, he would enliven the proceedings from time to time by turning sideways and shooting an impressively large missile into the heart of the flames. A direct hit resulted in a loud and satisfying sizzle. Naturally, with such skilled exponents of the art as role models, I'd vie with Geordie and Ian to see who could spit the furthest off any bridge over a burn. But it has to be admitted that ours were tame affairs by comparison, going badly wrong when we failed to judge the wind direction properly. Somehow the old mannies never did.

Given that this source of attraction was located close to our daily route to school, the proceedings on mart day were an irresistible lure. Even if the bustle of buying and selling the nowt might be over for the day by the time we trudged back up the road, there was still the interest of the loading of the remaining livestock into the departing fleet of floats. During the school holidays, we could hang about the place to our hearts' content, enjoying the day's steer-up. With all the frenzy of activity, and the three of us having a lot of growing still to do, we probably weren't really noticed and, provided we did nothing to get on the wrong side of the mart men, we seemed to be a tolerated presence.

The mart itself was a brown creosoted wooden structure surrounded by a maze of interconnecting wooden pens in which farm livestock awaited their moment of stardom in the auction ring. The building was like nothing else, being built in a circular shape around the ring. There was a hint of the interior of a kirk about it, in that it was arranged in stepped wooden benches in the manner of long pews where the farmers could sit and enjoy a view of the proceedings. The ones intent on serious business stood around the sides of the ring, nodding, winking, and scratching their nose or whatever their own particular signal to the auctioneer might be. It was sometimes difficult to see who was actually doing the bidding but the unctioneer, as everybody called him, knew exactly the signs to look for as he stood on his raised wooden dais, holding sway like a minister in the pulpit. When the bidding stopped, he brought his well-worn stick smartly down on the ledge. What exactly he was saying during the high speed conduct of the sale was a total mystery. As far as I was concerned, he might have been speaking in tongues but the farmers seemed to have a perfect understanding of this curious mart spik. The livelier the bidding, the more riveting the auctioneer's choreography became and his body language conveyed a wealth of detail.

We knew that buying and selling was an all-important matter and stayed well out of the way on the higher tiered seating where our giggling was absorbed into the roof space. It was as well to be as far removed as possible from the actual buying as 'everybody knew' that if you as much as put a hand to your nose you could end up being sold a stirk you couldn't pay for, and then there would be real trouble. Or so we believed, and thus we steadfastly avoided any potentially eye-catching movements – just in case. The loftiest seating was occupied only during exceptionally large sales and, as we slid back and fore along rows that had been smoothed by generations of farmers' bottoms (they would have had a less genteel word for them), our own doups acquired a thick grey coating of deposited stue.

From our lofty vantage point, it was like looking down on a theatrical performance as a steady flow of cows, sheep and pigs came and went from the nearby pens for selling. As they made their entry into the ring, the weight of each animal or small group was indicated in hundredweights on a huge clock with one big hand that could be easily seen by the potential buyers. (In the language of the place it was hunnerwechts that were spoken about). Also inside the ring, one of the mart attendants with a stick persuaded a beast to turn this way or that so that key details could be noted. With any luck, a sharp prod in a bullock's buttocks would provoke the show of prancing and kicking that we always hoped for, and the three of us fairly lapped up the performance as an excited animal squared up to the attendant and made him run for the side. The show may not have been quite as spectacular as the 'bucking broncos' we were familiar with in the Westerns at the Saturday afternoon cinema matinees, but while it cost a tanner to get into the picters, this local brand of Wild West entertainment was entirely free.

I don't recall any animosity towards us but should any of us fall foul of one of the mart men, the threat of expulsion was deterrent enough. We were free to wander about among the pens, stopping to look at tiny calves with misty eyes and long lashes that lay snugly among the straw, or at a well-horned beast that wouldn't have disgraced a Desperate Dan cow pie. We gave these well endowed specimens a wide berth since sharp-pointed horns could easily poke out through the spars. However, it was hard to resist the temptation of reaching an arm through the wooden slats of a pig pen and touching the occupant's hairy ear to make it grunt. Mind you, we saw this ploy backfire completely one day, thanks to a huge old sow which didn't appreciate the indignity of a squeezed lug and knew exactly how to get her own back. If Geordie had stuck to our usual practice of merely touching, all would have been well, but when he gave the nearest bristly lug a tight squeeze, the sow let out a high-pitched and prolonged squealing. As she continued with her exaggerated squeals, we decided it was time to beat a hasty retreat, avoiding eye contact with the mart men and trying to look as if a sweetie wouldn't melt in our mouths. As we slunk away, the old sow looked like she was settling back into the straw with a piggy smile of satisfaction under her hairy pink snout.

It was at the mart that we learned how expressive the spoken language of the North-east can be, albeit that the air was sometimes at the bluer end of the linguistic spectrum. To young ears, the range of oaths and blasphemies added even more to the attraction of the place. Should one of the mart men experience several hundredweights of cow bearing down on his foot from a misplaced hoof, the resultant outburst was a complete delight. Our teacher would have been horrified had she known that her charges were exposed to such colourful vocabulary. If anything, the air around the pens became even bluer when a beast failed to negotiate the wooden ramp leading up into a cattle float. If the over-excited creature should turn and charge off in the opposite direction, a blue posse of loudly cursing stick waving, dungaree-clad mart men would set off in hot pursuit, waving their sticks in the manner of the Keystone Cops.

The best entertainment we ever had came at the end of the day's selling when a wayward black bullock decided that it didn't fancy going into a float and made off completely from the premises. Naturally, this was too good an opportunity to miss and the three of us joined in the chase, shouting at the fleeing beast along with the mart men, determined to miss none of the excitement till the escapee was driven back to the mart. But the beast had other ideas and managed to avoid its pursuers completely, making its way into the main street. Terrified shoppers in head squares raced with their baskets of eerans for the safety of shop entrances as the fugitive pranced its way along the street, stopping the cars and bringing commerce to a halt. Naturally, we were sorry when the show came to an end and its star performer was chased back in the direction of the mart but we were all agreed that we'd never had such fun as we did that day when chaos satisfyingly reigned for a while in the heart of our normally placid burgh. Even the famed bull running at Pamplona would have been hard pushed to match the excitement for us, with traffic grinding to a halt in the street and skirling wifies diving for cover into doorways.

The summer months brought a welcome evening addition to the mart entertainment. On a set day of the week, an event advertised as a 'displenish sale' was held on the mart premises. When anybody did use its proper name, they referred to it as a displeenish but generally knew it as a roup. In the post-war years, these sales of second-hand goods were a main way of acquiring reasonably priced furniture and other household effects. Sometimes the items had been removed from a house clearance of some deceased old person. Though they were functional events, roups were highly entertaining as well, not to mention an opportunity for social comment. "Peer aul body; ye wid hae thocht she micht hae left mair nor that, an her abeen ninety" was the sort of remark passed as some nonagenarian's entire worldly goods were put on display, the object of public scrutiny and comment. Some, with no intention of buying a thing, just turned up to cast their eye over the deceased person's effects "oot o plain ull faschiouns," as folk said. The same men who sold the cattle in the ring by day tackled the roups at night. Not only could they conduct an effective sale, but they had a line of patter that drew folk in for the entertainment alone. Naturally, the place had to be spruced up a bit for these evening events but, while the worst of the animal deposits had been hosed away, a strong background smell of sharn still pervaded the air. Nevertheless, for lots of folk it was a pleasant way to pass a summer evening and there was always the chance of getting a bargain of something that nobody else wanted.

The auctioneers were well skilled in keeping folk entertained and certain items were guaranteed to be the butt of their humour. In particular, it was a time when more and more people were enjoying the luxury of a proper flush toilet. The result seemed to be an inordinate number of redundant china chamber pots, as often as not in bold Victorian patterns with colourful bunches of roses and such like on the side. They'd be worth a bob or two today, no doubt, as containers for plants, or even for something in which to mix a punch at a fancy party, but at the time they were of more value at a roup as a subject for a bit of joking and ribaldry. The patter might be something like: "Foo muckle am I bid for this bonnie chuntie? Maybe a wee bittie chippit at ae side, bit it wid be a gweed fit for somebody for a that - jist the thing for a winter's nicht if ye dinna want tae gyang ben a caul lobby."

Roups supplied a range of useful items. Redundant glass accumulator jars for old style radios went for a penny or so and were useful for housing tadpoles. They were a good source of second hand bikes and that's where mine came from. But a bike was a mundane object indeed compared to a faded and moth-eaten, mounted tiger's head that once came up for bidding. Doubtless it had graced the wall of some grand house in the Victorian age but now the once proud beast had fallen on hard times, stuck on top of a box of cracked and chipped old plates, baring its fangs harmlessly at the cobweb-covered roof beams. When it was held up to view there was a ripple of laughter at the thought that anybody would have any particular use for a stuffed tiger's head in their council house or prefab and the auctioneer struggled to coax out a starting bid. I felt really sorry for it as it seemed such a sad ending to a magnificent creature that had once padded stealthily around some eastern jungle; knocked down at a sharny-smelling cattle mart for the undignified sum of a penny. I would have loved to take it home as I felt so sorry for the body-less beast. Besides, what fun there could have been hiding behind a dyke and scaring unsuspecting quines with its snarling face.

Chapter 5: Flight of the turkeys

We never meant to let the turkeys loose. It all started on a cold afternoon a week or so before Christmas on the way back from school, when I stopped with Ian and Geordie beside a high and much creosoted wooden fence that we passed every day not far from home. But this time there was a bit of added interest. The unmistakable sound of a whole lot of gobbling turkeys was lifting up over the fence in the clear frosty air. It wasn't a sound you'd hear every day. As yet, the habit of consuming the birds for Christmas hadn't really caught on; well, not round our way anyway. When it came to seasonal eating, a well-fattened hen or cockerel off one of the nearby farms was more normal festive fare. Farm folk often trussed them up, wrapped them in thick brown paper tied up with string and sent them off in the post to relatives who lived at a distance. By the time they arrived at their final destination, the carcases were often sliding about in body juices, threatening to make an unscheduled exit at any minute from their wrappings in the postie's bag. Besides, New Year was the time for our winter celebration, not Christmas. To tell the truth, Christmas day wasn't very different from any other, with shops open for business and postal deliveries as normal.

For the three of us on our country rambles it was nothing out of the ordinary to see the occasional bubbly jock in a farmyard, puffed up with pride and parading with its grand tail fanned out behind. In fact, when it came to pride, not many birds could hold a candle to an inflated, red-faced turkey cock in full display. It must have been a particularly macho thing that made them go to all the bother of putting on such a show-off performance to impress their more slim-line females. They certainly made a speciality of fending off anyone who had the temerity to enter their territory. In particular, they seemed to have a particular dislike of people of my size, as I well knew from one particular farmyard. I could never relax any time I went there. As soon as I climbed over the heavy wooden gate, the old resident turkey cock would bear down in my direction, rustling his stiff tail feathers and looking like he meant business. Sensing fear on my part, the bird would quiver his tail even more and advance menacingly towards my bare legs, his bright red wattle dangling like a ridiculous floppy ornament above a sharp-pointed beak. It was the same with the testosterone-charged roosters that lorded it over their harems of hens, while the big white ganders were even worse with their noisy show of hissing and leg nipping. Fearing for my bare legs, I tended to give all of them a bit of a wide berth. But the tale involving the turkeys; well, that was a different thing altogether.

The high wooden fence had been so saturated in creosote over the years that it had taken on an almost black colouring and we sometimes paused to take a sniff at it on a warm summer's day when the smell came off in waves. Freshly spread tar had the same effect and some folk believed the fumes were beneficial in the bronchial department. Once, when the roadmen were tarring a bit of road near our house from an old tarry biler, our old neighbour, who was taking satisfaction in filling his lungs with the bitumen-infused air, advised me:"Snuff it up ma loon. It's gweed for ye!" Because the fence was conveniently endowed with knot holes at different heights, the three of us were able to see what was inside the enclosed yard. With one eye each to a different peep hole, we could see the long black shed in which the turkeys had been shut away from prying eyes, awaiting the arrival of the executioner, aka the plucker, who would thraw their necks before relieving them of their feathers. The prospect of taking a closer look was too much of a temptation and so off the three of us trooped down the side lane to see if we could get a peek inside the shed. Checking to see that there was nobody around, we tried the gate into the yard. To our satisfaction, it swung open easily on its big rusty hinge. People were more trusting then; you didn't have gangs of pre-Christmas turkey rustlers going around the countryside in vans, relieving farms of several hundred Christmas dinners at a time.

The shed's tiny windows were too high up for anyone of our limited stature to reach and so, feeling quite daring, we stood aside while Geordie quietly lifted the wooden latch and slowly pushed the door open. In the dimly lit interior, we could make out a couple of dozen anxious looking birds. When the door creaked open further, they suddenly fell silent and craned their necks from side to side to stare at their unexpected visitors. We may not have been very big but, to the turkeys, we were still representatives of the human race and therefore to be viewed with the deepest suspicion, bearing in mind the season of year. Perhaps they were thinking that their time was now up. At any rate, we stood and stared at them and they stared back at us in an uncomfortable silence.

Suddenly the spell broke. "That's the mannie comin!" shouted Ian and Geordie in unison, a touch of panic in their voices, as the wind stirred the branches of the big sycamore tree outside. The heavy wooden door banged shut and we took to our heels up the lane, little thinking that when we pushed the door open we might have opened a Pandora's Box. At some point later the wind must have let the unfastened door swing open. Clearly, the birds weren't as daft as they looked and half a dozen of the sharper witted among them had seized the moment to make a flight for freedom. When we came past next morning, a few passers-by were stopping to look up at the topmost branches of the tree. Some were shaking their heads in disbelief, others having a good laugh. As they paused to gawk up at the high flying turkeys, the escaped birds gawked back down at them, a look of suspicion in their beady eyes, cocking their heads from one side to the other. Through the knot holes we could see an extremely irate individual with a long wooden pole, making unsuccessful attempts to persuade one of the black silhouettes to come down from the tree. We could tell he was hopping mad by the look on his face and by the language that went with each wielding of the stick. But all the cajoling, threatening and swearing was to no avail; the birds clearly weren't going to descend, at least not quite yet.

These were no turkey-brained dafties. They were the old fashioned type, much closer to the original wild breed than today's massive, overweight, artificially inseminated creations that have been specially bred just to sit about, do nothing but eat and put on ever more oven weight. No way were these individuals with the embedded guile of their forbears going to give in to a quick surrender to the plucker down below and part with their plumage for the sake of somebody's dinner. Cold or no cold, they would just fluff out their feathers and stick it out on their draughty perches. The scene beyond the fence resembled a prison roof-top demonstration, with the passers-by shaking their heads at the wayward ways of turkeys. Slightly shamefacedly, the three of us looked at one another, then at the birds, knowing full well what had happened. Only they and we knew who had engineered the great escape; that we were the ones who'd sprung the jail birds and released them from death row. When we ran off that time, the shed door had closed all right but the sneck was undone and the rest, as they say, was history. On the way home from school that afternoon we looked in vain for the turkeys as we trudged through the snow that had fallen earlier in the day. Perhaps cold and hunger had finally proved too much and they'd come down and surrendered to their fate. I kept my head down when mention was made at home of the tale of the fugitive birds. By this time, the story involved some kind of mass breakout, involving goodness knows how many dozens of birds.

But I knew better, and said nothing when the subject was mentioned, nursing a few guilt feelings about my part in what had happened.

In those days just before Christmas, when the turkeys and their feathers were fated to part company, we invariably stopped on our way back home to look at the well-filled glass jars in the sweetie shop window and speculate on which ones we would buy if we had the money. In keeping with the season, the window was brightly lit, well stocked and decorated with fake snow consisting of wads of fluffy white cotton wool along with sparkling silver tinsel. "I like that black an fyte eens the best" said Ian, eyeing up a well-filled jar of striped humbugs and drooling at the mouth at the thought of getting his hands on the whole lot. "I canna stick at eens," I added, pointing to a jar of the green boilings called soor plooms. "Aye," added Geordie in agreement, screwing up his face, "they're maist hellafa soor fan ye sook them." I agreed; they were definitely not my favourites. The choice on the shelves was seemingly endless. Tiny dolly mixtures kept company with shiny black liquorice allsorts, while jelly babies rubbed shoulders with multicoloured flat motto lozenges bearing printed messages. In small cardboard boxes at the front, sticks of rhubarb rock in purple and green wrappings and sherbet fountains in short yellow tubes were strategically placed to tempt passing youngsters. Sweets were not that common at home and were regarded by my granny as an indulgence. She firmly believed that too much sweet stuff wasn't good for the stomach and had her own name for things in the sweetie line. "Ower muckle smacherie's nae gweed for a body's stamack," she would say. So, there wasn't much chance of getting rotten teeth in our house.

The shop didn't have the monopoly in sweet things, however. Along the road, at the baker's window, we stood in awe of monumental, three-tiered wedding cakes on silver stands, each layer covered over with frilly bits of white icing and adorned here and there with swirls of pink or blue, and with little bride and bridegroom figures stuck on the top. Apart from the almost constant display of specially ordered wedding cakes, I really liked the way the window displays were made to reflect the different seasons. Earlier in the year, tiny yellow chickens adorned a range of fancy Easter cakes. Then, with the tinted leaves of autumn falling from the trees, the window took on a fresh seasonal look with fancy marzipan apples and beautifully crafted marzipan leaves in autumnal shades of yellow and orange. In the weeks before Christmas, it was the turn of fat robin redbreasts and red-cheeked Santas to brighten the white iced surfaces. The hand-painted sign above the door bore the description 'Baker and Confectioner' and the confectionery side of things was certainly an eye-catching feature of the business.

The everyday incidents of life provided us with no end of entertainment. We drew in our breath as cats took it into their heads to risk one of their nine lives by making a daring dash across the road among car wheels. We laughed at men trying to start their cars with a freezing cold starting handle on a winter's morning and getting a kick back from the thing when the engine suddenly started into life, and it afforded us infinite amusement to see customers who were the worse for drink outside the pubs giving voice to maudlin songs and swaying unsteadily on their feet on icy pavements. We could also rely, at some point during the week, on meeting up with our friend, the coalman's horse. On the coldest days he sported a faded green winter canvas coat to match his moo bag as he pulled the laden coal cart through the snow.

Our route took us close by the smiddy, a place of guaranteed interest. It was no great detour to pass the open yard with its clutter of rusty agricultural ironmongery brought in for repair over the years and for various reasons left unclaimed. Close by, stood the patient work horses that had been brought in from the farms for shoeing. No horse boxes then; most of the gentle beasts were led in by halter, clopping their way along the busy street. Sometimes you'd even see a man or an orra loon astride one of the horses. As the dungaree-clad knights rode by on their big chargers with the big hooves ringing on the street, they hardly raised a second glance since it was still a familiar scene, though in sharp decline.

It wasn't just the horses that drew us to the place but the sounds and smell of a busy working smiddy. Just inside the door, the blacksmith, in worn leather apron, lorded it over his fiery domain. The beads of sweat on his brow shone in the glow of the fire as sparks took to the air each time he poked and prodded among the heat of the furnace. When a glowing red shoe was lifted out on long tongs and placed on the anvil, the ringing of hammer upon metal echoed about the yard, a sound retained in my memory as a reminder of a farming age now gone. Of course, there are farriers who move about the countryside in vans these days, putting new shoes on to horses and ponies that are kept purely for pleasure. But it was the giant, hard working beasts patiently waiting their turn in the smiddy yard that we loved to go and see.

They came in all shades of brown and white and grey, the Clydesdales that were still working on the land despite the advancing tide of tractors. To prepare for shoeing, the blacksmith lifted back the animal's leg and held it firmly against his apron as he cut away at the hoof with a sharp knife. The strong smell of singeing horse hoof pervaded the air as the red hot shoe was applied. "Gyad, fit an affa stink" the three of us would complain at the moment when the hot shoe came into contact with the hoof. Things were at their worst when the odour was trapped in the cold air of a winter's afternoon and we would make a show of holding our noses. But it never stopped us looking in by the smiddy time and time again and thoroughly enjoying the experience.

Clydesdales have made a bit of a come-back these days but they tend to feature at shows where the flowing hair on their lower legs gets the talcum powder treatment and hours are spent pampering and preparing them for the judge's eye. No longer are they called upon to perform useful tasks behind plough or coup-cairt as their ancestors did on the old style farms, and no longer do streets resound to the metallic clop of horse hooves on their way to be shod. The working beasts have long gone and the fascinating, old-fashioned, cluttered, noisy, smelly smiddies with them.

Chapter 6: Brushes with wifies

The women who lived round our way were all quite old. At least, that's how I thought of them at the time; it's just the way you imagine things when you're young. I suppose the reality was that our married female neighbours dressed much the same and did the same sort of things with their lives, which was pretty much to run the household and bring up a family. Individuality in attire was definitely not the order of the day. And supposing they had the money (which they didn't) there wasn't the availability and range of fashion clothes for them to make themselves look very different anyway. After all, it wasn't long before that you'd needed coupons to buy clothes, and pairs of nylons had been as scarce as hens' teeth. In my mind, 'fashion' and 'glamour' were words associated with film stars at the picter hoose and definitely not with our female neighbours.

Today's fashion conscious world is awash with hair salons offering the latest in styles but the women I'm talking about here attended to their own coiffure, from time to time letting some neighbour loose on their heads for a haircut involving a pair of sharp scissors, or shears as we called them, then resorting to a well-filled box of curlers to put some life into their shorn locks. The latter metal items were designed to coerce hair into taking on a degree of curl that it wasn't inclined to do of its own accord, hence the name. When it was necessary to go outside the house, say to make a purchase from the baker's van, curlers were sometimes happit up with a head square for the sake of decorum, with only the front ones protruding, but some wifies went about with so much exposed metal work on their heads that they'd have been well advised not to venture out when there was thunder and lightning in the vicinity. Some of them employed a much bigger and lethal looking metal thing with a row of pointed teeth and a tight spring called a crocodile. It was well named and resembled more a mediaeval instrument of torture than any kind of fashion accessory. I suspect its inventor must have been some kind of sadist. Any archaeologist of the far future who unearths a long buried, rusting crocodile might well assume that it was some sort of rodent trap. By opening up the jaws with their fearsome set of teeth, hair could be forced into complete submission, this time creating a fashionable wave effect.

Almost none of our female neighbours went out to work, except on rare occasions when part-time labour was required. This happened at tattie liftin time when they would dress themselves up in their men's worn-out jackets and breeks, turn a head square into a turban and go out into the surrounding countryside in the autumn. Some farmers hired a bus from a local garage if they had quite a few acres of tatties to lift. As the wifies piled into the long-nosed, single cab Bedford buses they looked a right ticket. And when you heard them, they were worse than excited bairns, probably divulging saucy domestic secrets to one another, to judge by the high-pitched giggles and embarrassed red faces. It was back-breaking toil as they worked their way along the dreels, lifting the tatties and putting them into wire baskets called sculls in a park close to the road. It must have been the sheer sense of freedom in getting out of the house that made them so excited. Even if it happened to be in the clarty setting of a tattie park after a heavy shower of rain, it was a brief return to the carefree days before marriage came along and the responsibilities of bringing up a family of bairns overtook them.

For the rest of the time, their home was their castle. Some were immensely house proud, with a pride that extended out into their little bit of surrounding territory. Each house beside ours had a space at the back for a green with claes poles and tows for hanging the washing on. Narrow wooden stretchers with a knick at the top to catch the tow were used to hoist the washing up. Beside the washin green, the ground was used for growing tatties and assorted vegetables but the houses faced directly on to the street with no front garden to give a lift to the cheerless stone or grey harled walls. Even so, some of the more formidable among the wifies defended their front step and pavement as fiercely as nations defend their air space and anyone who treated their territory with anything less than respect could look out.

Doorsteps were washed and scrubbed with regularity and no ship's deck can have been more assiduously swabbed down than some of those front steps were. You could see the keenest of them of a morning, down on hands and knees with scrubbing brush and big block of green washing soap, scrubbing away in a froth of soapy suds till the stone fairly shone. In the ultimate makeover, doorsteps were anointed with a substance called Cardinal Red to give them a colourful spruce up. Even the pavement out in front was subjected to a constant brushing and slooshing with water to reduce the risk of any dirt being brought inside. Once into the lobby, the fresh atmosphere of the outdoors was replaced by an overpowering smell of floor polish that radiated from the shining linoleum. You had to be good at keeping your balance when you went into some houses. When a thin lobby mat lay on top of highly polished lino, it was like stepping on to the surface of an ice rink as the mat did its best to shoot away under your feet and you needed all your wits to concentrate on keeping upright. This arrangement of mat on top of polished lino was a perfect demonstration of the power of house pride over practicality.

Woe betide anybody bringing - horror of horrors - so much as a suggestion of dog's dirt to the door on their feet. Should this happen, a full scale emergency was declared, with bucket of boiling hot water, mop and powerfully smelling carbolic soap. In the worst case scenario, where somebody's dog had taken such a liking to that stretch of pavement that it was using it on a regular basis, a powerful wash of Jeyes Fluid was applied as the ultimate deterrent. The smell lingered for days and drifted into the lobby but, on the positive side, the canine that had done the dirty deed wasn't willing to hang around long enough to perform with that kind of smell hanging in the air.

Belonging to the band of housewives round our way meant donning the uniform that went with the role. For the purposes of full-scale step scrubbing, a tie-over, patterned pinafore was normal attire, often with a turban (a word suggestive of a scene more exotic than was actually the case). Just along the road from our house lived a woman much noted for spending her day hunting for stue about the house. It was said that she went about the place, duster in hand, waiting to pounce on any speck before it had a chance to settle. When she wasn't dusting, she spent so much time polishing her linoleum that it was a wonder she didn't rub the pattern off. She also took an inordinate proprietorial interest in the stretch of pavement in front of her house. Unfortunately, a smooth pavement like that was heaven sent to loons shod in tackety boots. The technique was much like being on a winter slide in the school playground, that's to say you could take a short run and enjoy a satisfying, if brief, glide across the smooth surface. A really accomplished slider gaining sufficient speed could even make sparks fly from the metal tackets on the soles, leaving white score marks behind on the surface.

Oblivious to the lurking danger, Geordie and I happened one Saturday morning to be intent on a bit of pavement sliding and were ill-advised enough to choose this particular stretch on which to do it. Just as we were sliding past, the green painted door suddenly opened and out the wifie flew like a futrat, sweeping brush in hand. We were probably too stunned by her turn of speed to make off fast enough, with the result that we both felt the end of her brush round our shins as we fled. "If ye dee that again, ye'll get yer heids in yer hans tae play wi!" she shouted after us. She also threatened to report us to our teacher if we repeated the offence. Now, that really was an effective deterrent, as teachers then doubled up as guardians of community behaviour by dealing with pupils in school for demeanours that had been committed outside. Needless to say, we chose our sliding places more judiciously after that.

That other maintainer of community discipline, the local bobby, wasn't averse either to a light bit of corporal chastisement of the young if he felt they deserved it. A bobby in uniform on the ground was nothing to remark upon; they often just wandered around the place, tuning in to useful bits and pieces of community on-goings as they went about in their high-collared dark blue tunics and diced caps. But when a police car came along, that really was worthy of comment. The white lace screens fairly twitched to see which house the black Maria was stopping at. Few scenes from a Western movie, with a gunslinger walking in a tense atmosphere down past the sheriff's office, could have been more gripping as all eyes focused on the scene from nearby windows. I think I always harboured a desire to see somebody we knew being lifted by the police and led away in shame in handcuffs but it never happened. It was just as likely that the bobbies had called at the house following a fa-oot among some inebriated neighbours, or somebody had reported the occupants for not having a dog licence. Still, while it lasted, it provided a brief bit of entertainment.

A uniformed sight that attracted much interest and comment was the arrival of the telegram delivery boy on his Post Office issue bike. In the war years, folk were familiar with the dread arrival of a small yellow envelope from a telegram boy with a little pill box hat on his head. The telegrams contained in their little leather wallets were the terse, soulless conveyors of news that a father, son or brother had been killed in action and would never be back with the family again. But the years had moved on and telegrams containing strips of messages that were ultra short and abbreviated for the sake of cost were now often the means of informing of a family death outwith the area since telephones were few and far between. Certainly, nobody we knew had one in their house.

They were a feisty lot, our neighbour wifies, fighting their corner when they needed to, and they were especially well practised in their disputes with the coalman. In addition to their long-running tirades against weet coal, there was the question of the quantity of stones contained in the sacks. As the horse waited patiently between the shafts, they would cite the exact number that had been revealed when they went to empty out their ais pans after cleaning out their grates in the morning. Some even came out with the pan, bearing the evidence among the grey ash. "A'm nae pyin for a lot o steens!" was the familiar response to the long suffering deliverer of fuel but it was hardly his fault. The miners who hacked away with their picks in the dark underground seams inevitably brought down stones as well as coal, and the washing process at the pit-head didn't always show up the non-combustible bits. Fortunately, the coalman had a back that was broad enough to accommodate both the heavy coal sacks and the haranguing. "That last lot o coal ye brocht wis nae eese," one dissatisfied customer would complain. "Nae eese ava!" her neighbours would intone in supportive unison, in the manner of a Greek chorus.

As far as burning the coal was concerned, there was no smoke without soot and herein lay a challenge. Bringing in the chimney sweep to clean a dirty lum meant shelling out money, so soot often built up and things were left to the very last minute, often with unintended and spectacular consequences. When somebody's lum gied up, as they said, a pall of acrid smoke from the burning soot hung over the area, following on from a spectacular show of flames leaping out of the cracking chimney can. Entertaining though this was to youngsters like myself, an event like this was far from pleasing to the neighbours as it meant shutting windows to keep out the choking smoke and, worse, if there was a washing out, having to rush outside, take down the stretcher and clear the washing line before everything was contaminated with the smoky smell or marked by black particles of descending soot.

On our way to and from school, we always thought it amusing when we saw a sooty round brush appear unexpectedly out of the top of a chimney can. As the brush turned round and round it looked like a spiky-haired black puppet and we knew that the sweep must be at work in the fireplace down below, giving somebody's chimney a professional clean. Sometimes we spotted an amateur sweep up on a roof, dropping a brush with a heavy metal ball down a chimney. This was another effective way of dislodging the soot but the all important thing was to ensure that it was the right chimney if there were several cans close together. A case of mistaken identity might result in the occupants down below getting a rude awakening when a cloud of black soot landed without warning round their feet as they sat having a fly cup by the fireside. Some folk laid claim to the soot after the sweep had done his work, scattering it along their rows of carrots to deter the dreaded carrot root fly which could wreak havoc with the crop and cause the ferny green foliage to collapse.

Human nature being what it was, not everybody believed in putting out good money in getting the sweep in, so a fair bit of DIY chimney cleaning went on and sets of sweeping brushes and the long rods to go with them were passed around among neighbours. There was, of course, the other option of pittin yer lum up, the time-honoured practice whereby you deliberately set your chimney on fire to effect a thorough, if more dramatic, cleaning. To create a fire as part of a planned strategy of conflagration, all that was required was to thrust some scrunched newspaper up the lum and set light to it. The rapidly burning paper caused the soot to burn and it wasn't long before things started to roar like something taking off from a Nasa launch pad. The end result of this semi-controlled fire raising was an instant improvement in the drawing quality of the fire, though there was a certain risk involved if the lum hadn't been swept for some time and went up with particular ferocity, causing somebody to call out the fire brigade. When the brigade arrived on the scene in their shiny red fire engine with brass bell ringing, they ran their flat canvas hose out and poured gallons of water down the lum, creating a soggy, sooty mess in the surrounds of the fireplace that took hours to clean up. Anybody who suffered the experience of having the brigade come to put a fire out in their lum was naturally careful to avoid the sotter, not to mention the shame, in future.

Chapter 7: At the picters

The picters, which is what we collectively called the local picture house and its featured films, had a great attraction for every age group in the place. In pre-TV times, the latest films with big name actors and actresses had a large following and a popular star could have the place packed out. If you took a look round the back of the premises, the picter hoose in which the glamorous stars featured was anything but a thing of beauty: a long, windowless, brick-built, unprepossessing box of a place where the aesthetics of architecture hadn't featured much in the builder's plans. But the other end was a different matter altogether; a hint of something more exotic in the midst of the ordinariness of everyday life. Here was a frontage like none other in town with its touches of art deco and an invite into the world of the silver screen. Flat glass display cases showing scenes of highest drama or deepest passion from the 'Now Showing' film and the 'Coming Attractions' adorned the front walls. Up the steps, doors with decorated glass panels opened on to a brightly lit foyer with its whiff of trapped cigarette smoke and kiosk where the lady who sold the small red and green tickets tore them off a long roll.

From my very first wide-eyed visit, the auditorium was a place apart. Its slightly mysterious inner sanctum was screened from the bright world outside by a thick red velvet curtain. Beyond the veil, the gatekeepers of the dimly lit interior were the usherettes in unflattering uniforms and matching pillbox hats. Tilting the latter slightly to one side was an effort to make them a touch more fashionable but it was a bit of a vain gesture; the headwear still managed to look more daft than decorative in our kind of setting. Each of these servant maidens of the inner chamber carried a torch with a beam strong enough to guide you down the downward sloping aisle and direct you into your seat, since the inside was totally black except for the feeble pink glow from a few shell-shaped lamps stuck against the walls.

They were a grim faced lot, the usherettes, who made it abundantly clear that they had little time for minors who'd only paid a tanner to get in to the Saturday matinee. To be fair, their unfortunate expressions and unprepossessing looks might have had a lot to do with the fact that you only saw their faces lit up by torchlight from below. Inevitably, this tended to accentuate their less alluring features, like nostrils and moustaches. No wonder there was an air of tension among them when we all trooped in through the doors on a Saturday afternoon: a ragbag mob of keyed-up kids with sweaty sixpenny bits clutched in our hands, ready for the matinee to commence. You could see the usherettes surveying the incoming hordes, passing whispered comments to one another about the less desirable looking among us, the ones they'd picked out by intuition and experience as potential troublemakers and would need to be watched. I daresay anyone would have been snippy and apprehensive when dozens of noisy, animated kids arrived in a mob all at once; a certain recipe for trouble. The poor souls probably had sleepless nights every Friday at the mere imagining of what might ensue the next day.

Once we'd been relieved of our money, we filed towards the curtained entrance where one of the usherettes took our tickets with ill grace and tore them in half. The atmosphere in the Stygian gloom was a heady mix of stale tobacco smoke and cheap scent. Perhaps it was as well that you never saw the place in proper light. The walls must have been brown with nicotine staining owing to the fact that a large proportion of film goers were smokers. In fact, the place had even been designed with the needs of the nicotine addicted in mind. In between every pair of seats was a conveniently positioned metal ashtray which, by the end of an evening performance, could be overflowing with fag ends. Air conditioned the place most certainly was not. To counteract the fug and general sweatiness of the atmosphere the auditorium received an occasional freshen-up, not by opening windows since there weren't any, but by the action of the usherettes. In times of need, they sprayed an air freshener into the air from gold coloured pump-action sprayers. If you happened to be sitting in one of the aisle seats, you could feel the stuff descending around you like a fine mist.

The distinctive picture house atmosphere also owed something to the strong scent worn by young women who'd come with their boyfriends and sat and canoodled in the back seats. There was, however, a price to be paid for the picture house passion. The Lotharios of the place had to be prepared to put their hands in their pockets and stump up a bit extra for tickets for the back seats under the balcony since that was the recognised zone for that kind of thing. If I ever had the good luck to be taken to an evening performance, a rare occurrence, it was to the cheaper seats we went. You could go home with a sore neck from looking up to the screen if the place was busy and you'd been shown to one of the seats right down near the front. The balcony, with the dearest seats, was decidedly *terra incognita* as far as I was concerned. On the way out at the end of a film, I sometimes managed a good look at a bit of serious passion in the back stalls, because occasionally a couple of smoochers had got so carried away with their amorous activities that they never noticed the lights going up, let alone that everybody else had been standing up around them for the national anthem, leaving them lost in their own world, entwined in a passionate embrace.

Romance, in its widest sense, was what the world of the cinema was all about; an escape from the down to earth reality of life in the day to day world outside and a chance to see favourite stars in action. The foyer walls were hung with large black and white photo portraits of the best known heartthrobs, each of whom had a following. Big Hollywood personalities like Rita Hayworth, Jayne Mansfield, Clark Gable and Gregory Peck gazed lovingly down upon their fans with big Hollywood smiles and sparkling teeth that must have cost countless dollars in dental bills to maintain in their whiter than white, perfect condition. Their pictures, signed across the bottom with sprawling signatures as exotic looking as their owners, shared the hanging space with stars of the cowboy films, like Roy Rodgers in his white ten gallon hat. It never occurred to me at the time to wonder at the practicality of going around in a hat that colour with all that dirt being thrown into the air by galloping horse hooves.

It was hardly any wonder that I was often involved in gunfight scenarios involving my co-gunslingers, Geordie and Ian. We were, all three of us, the proud possessors of a gun and holster, like most loons of our age. We engaged in makkie-on shoot-outs from behind a wall or round the gavel of a house since cowboy films were the stuff of the Saturday matinees and the cowboys had become our role models. Sharing the silver screen with the cowpokes were the likes of Laurel and Hardy, the Three Stooges and Old Mother Reilly. We laughed at the antics of Laurel and Hardy trying to move a piano upstairs, or one of the trio we called the 'Three Stoogies' having a finger forever poked into his eye by one of the others. It was some years later before I realised that 'stooge' was actually a dictionary word and had a meaning; I just thought it was what the comedy trio were called. Cowboy favourites like Hopalong Cassidy and the smooth looking Roy Rodgers (not forgetting his highly intelligent horse, Trigger), with wide leather chaps, silver spurs and fancy guns, had immense appeal and came out unscathed every time, no matter how much trouble they were in. After all, their presence was required on screen again next week or the week after. We never tired of seeing Westerns but they were responsible for bringing the most charged atmosphere to the place. As the smart mounted guys in blue from the US Cavalry got themselves trapped in a dry gulch and the menacing outline of the Injuns appeared on the skyline above, we knew that trouble was brewing and that a gunfight was on the cards. Smoke signals on the skyline spelled certain trouble. Amidst a chorus of whooping from charging Redskins, the attack would begin in earnest as both dry gulch and picture house echoed to gunfire. Somehow there always just happened to be the most convenient of big boulders for the shooters to hide behind, a safe place to dodge the bullets that whined and ricocheted all around. Camera shots went from our cowboy hero taking careful aim with his Colt, or whatever shooting iron he drew out of his holster, to the recipient of his perfectly aimed bullet who staggered back and was no more. We cheered to the rafters the fight-back of the brave Cavalry men and joined in a chorus of hissing and booing when the Indian braves launched their counter attack. Little did I realise then how much of a diet of biased pap we were being fed, week in week out. When it came to what we were meant to think about America's first native people, no communist state intent on indoctrinating its youth could have been more successful than the makers of those Saturday afternoon Westerns.

The atmosphere became quite electric when a good going gunfight was at its height, and this was precisely the time when trouble could ensue. A break in a section of worn celluloid film at a critical point in a Saturday afternoon Western must have been the ultimate dread of the usherette brigade and the main reason they probably couldn't get a proper sleep the night before. As the sweating projectionist in his airless box at the back of the balcony wrestled with the big reel and attended to the tear in the film, things were in danger of getting seriously out of hand. Now it was the turn of the usherettes to find themselves caught up in a battle zone as they rushed up and down the aisles like demented hens, trying to quell the riot, their only weapons the shrill voices, which they used like harridans, and their torches which they flashed at us like snipers, firing at the worst of the miscreants with accusing beams of light. The noise level at such moments had to be heard to be believed and it took a good five minutes after the film got going again for the turmoil to subside completely. If truth be told, things never did quite return to where they'd been. In the snapping of the film reel, the spell had somehow been broken and there was no going back.

Even when things were going reasonably well, there was still scope for trouble to break out. Youngsters in my age group would never have dared try a fag but it was possible to buy a cinnamon stick for a penny or less at a nearby shoppie and some loons came armed with a box of matches and tried a puff or two of that. The smell of singeing cinnamon was truly awful and further enraged the usherettes, who couldn't always pinpoint the source of the offending fumes. With their own war cry of "Pit **that** oot or I'll pit **you** oot!" they fixed accusing stares on anybody sitting in the general direction of the offending smell. Older loons who'd managed to filch the odd fag from their father's Woodbine packet at home puffed away with impunity in the darkness as the smoke, along with the dust raised by stamping feet, rose up into the blue beam of the projected film. Bits of paper flicked from elastic bands became bright missiles as they caught the projected light and sailed through the air. The longer the break took to repair, the worse things became, with loud whistling from the older ones who'd perfected the art with two fingers in the mouth, and with impatient foot stamping all round. In the worst case scenarios the worn-out film got going again, only to start slipping and to stop once more, a situation that fuelled the unrest even further and must have made the usherettes contemplate laying down their torches in instant surrender.

Just to make sure everybody came back the next week, the weekly instalment of the serial always ended on a nail biting note. At the last critical minute somebody was about to be scalped by an Indian, a full-rigged man o' war on the high seas was about to be boarded by pirates who'd just run up the scary black skull and crossbones flag above their mainsail, or some hapless female was being tied to a railroad track by an evil looking baddie as a puffing steam locomotive with box car behind came thundering towards her at a rate of knots. It was all gripping stuff and, needless to say, what had seemed like certain doom and death was averted at the very start of the next episode.

The effect of all this was to induce a form of hyperactivity verging on mass hysteria. A particularly gripping scenario had its impact for hours afterwards, starting with the moment we came blinking out of the blackness of the cinema into the light of afternoon, like a crowd of stirks let out of a byre on to new spring grass. On the way home, the three of us would clap one hand against our side, with the other holding on to imaginary reins in front: make-believe gunslingers urging make-believe horses on to ever greater speed. We galloped along the pavements, stopping now and again to fire at one another with pointed index and next finger, making shooting noises from the corners of buildings. For authenticity, we had the benefit of the vocabulary we'd picked up inside. One of us would point a pistol at the others, making loud shooting noises and shouting defiantly "Tak that, ye varmints!" Or, we would run along the top of the low walls in front of houses, risking the wrath of the residents and have them rapping on their windows at us as we jumped from imaginary ship to ship where there was a gap in their wall, or fought a noisy, swashbuckling battle on the pavement outside with invisible cutlasses.

There was one last down side to the picters that I probably shouldn't forget to mention. It used to be said of the cinema in the old days, that you could "gyang in wi a freen an cam oot wi stranger." The friend would be visible enough but the stranger might not make its presence known till you'd gone to bed afterwards and felt a distinct itch. "Mak certain sure ye dinna cam hame wi a flech!" was my granny's weekly warning as I set off for the matinee, though how I could have done anything about it was another matter. In the matter of the Doric language, there are many complications for outsiders, and one of them is that fleas are flechs and the flies that buzz about in summer are flees. The fact was that fleas could be part of community living in those days if you happened to mix with company from a background of sub-standard housing and dubious personal hygiene. There were still children in our school whose parents were squatters, taking up residence in redundant wartime huts and similar unoccupied premises in the absence of proper housing, and such places were under suspicion as a breeding ground for that less than desirable form of wildlife. A decade or so later, when I was a student, I went to the real live flea circus in the Tivoli Gardens in Copenhagen and saw a woman with a whole lot of flechs that earned their keep by performing after they'd been allowed to feed on her arm. I may have been in Denmark but my mind instantly drifted back across the North Sea to those Saturday matinees.

The picters provided us with an escape into worlds that were far removed from the one in which we lived, where the distinctions between good and bad were always completely clear cut. But, looking back on it now, I realise the extent to which truth and reality were decidedly skewed at times in our weekly fix of gun-slinging Westerns.

Chapter 8: Potted heid and hairy tatties

Some things are the stuff of gastronomic nightmares. How hairy tatties got their name isn't hard to fathom if you've ever had to consume any. Apart from the tattie side of things, the main ingredient of a dish that was once traditional North-east fare, and one which was over-enthusiastically embraced by my granny, was codfish. But should this conjure up a vision of an appetising specimen of the species enrobed in crispy beer batter accompanying a portion of chips, I should erase it now.

I've no doubt the fish would have been recognisable enough as a cod when it swam the North Sea, but before it made the journey to our house via the fish man's less than fragrant van, it had been caught, split and laid out to dry for weeks in the open air, doubtless with a squadron of bluebottles in attendance. By this time, it had been thoroughly salted and had now taken on the look and consistency of anaemic cardboard, only it was much more solid and still had a recognisable fish's tail. Edibility was not a word that sprung readily to mind while viewing a piece of dried cod that looked as if it might substitute for a bat in a table tennis game. My heart sank into a state of real scunner every time I saw my granny carry one of the hard white slabs into the house from the fish man's van because I knew that a plateful of hairy tatties would undoubtedly follow.

I should perhaps tread carefully at this point in case a Norwegian friend of mine might chance to read this and think I'm being uncomplimentary about the love in his life. Now a distinguished professor of marine biology, his life's passion has been cod, or rather the tapeworms that take up residence and cadge free board and lodging in their interiors. When he and I shared a room as university researchers, I got quite used to seeing his tapeworm collection sitting about in tall jars on the window sill: peelie-wally threads of parasite, pickled for posterity in crystal clear spirit. Dried cod is a famed product of his kinsmen and a source of pride in his country, though what happens to the tapeworms in the process of desiccation I'm none too sure. The Norwegians who fish the chilly waters of the north have always gone in for cod drying in a big way, sending it off to faraway Africa where it travels well in the tropical heat. I learned this fact much later; had I known it when it was standard fare at home, I'd have been more than happy to forego my portions of hairy tatties in favour of feeding faraway Africans who might have appreciated it more.

Anyway, the urge came upon my granny with unfortunate regularity to set about creating a great panful of the stuff. Following its overnight soaking in a pail of water, and in resemblance now to a more soggy form of cardboard, the fish began to swell until it took on a new appearance, one that was no more recognisable as a cod nor more appetising looking than before. The culinary result of this union of cooked cod and potato kirned up in the pot was hairy tatties. Since those days, I've often eaten salt cod prepared by a French friend with potato, olive oil and garlic in the warm, lavender-scented air of Provence and found it nothing short of delicious, but the phrase *haute cuisine* somehow doesn't sit easily alongside memories of a plateful of my granny's hairy tatties.

The 'hairy' nature of this dish derived from the over-abundant softened bones among the tattie component. I used to think that if live cod swimming in the sea had to move around with that number of bones, it was a wonder they ever managed to get anywhere. Once you popped a forkful into your mouth the softened bones were everywhere, sticking between your teeth and tickling the roof of your mouth.

In contrast to his decrepit green-painted van with its starting handle sticking out in front of the radiator, the fish man was a spry looking character with a shiny red face and shiny brown leather leggings to match. He looked very fit - "A swack kin o chiel," my granny would have said. Like the seagulls that left the coast to seek shelter in our inland howe in stormy weather, he came from a faraway world and seemed to bring a breath of sea air with him. But, unlike the gulls, he came on a set day and blew a shrill whistle to announce his presence. There was something of the equine about his unusual leg wear. At some time in the past he maybe had a horse and cart and hadn't quite made the transition in attire to reflect his motorised mode of transport. When he flung open the doors at the back of the van, it was to reveal an array of open wooden fish boxes with the Aberdeen fish merchants' names stencilled in black paint along the sides. As soon as his shrill whistle was blown, the wifies went out with their plates and purses. For weighing out the fish he had an old set of scales with metal weights that he placed on and off until the two sides came into balance. There was never any suggestion of wrapping; a flat plate carried out to the van received the purchases straight off the scales. For preference, the fish was cooked on the day the van came, since nobody had a fridge and the smell wasn't something that you wanted to hang about the house.

I looked forward to the visits from the fish man. Looking into the back of his van was like peering into an aquarium with the water taken out, a place where all manner of fascinating creatures of the deep reposed. They appeared calm in death but some specimens sported sets of teeth so sharp that it was obvious they'd been a force to contend with in the days of their living. Some looked as though they weren't dead at all and when the fish man was preoccupied in chat, I sometimes cautiously reached out my hand to touch an array of fearsome teeth, ready to draw back if I suddenly thought the owner might have a bit of life still in it. When I gazed in awe on a massive conger eel, I wondered how anybody could have the courage to eat such a scary looking beast. Though he maybe didn't realise it, the fish man was providing me with an enlightening weekly marine biology lesson.

The fish that were laid out for scrutiny in the back of the van came into two main categories: fresh and smoked. Haddock and cod were firm favourites and so were long pieces of ling. Herrings were cheap and appeared in the same sleek and silvery form as when they were shaken out of the nets of the steam drifters that very morning. Though long departed this life, they still managed to swim around, this time in a sea of bree, a richly smelling substance that sometimes found its way out of the boxes and seeped out through the gap under the van's ill-fitting back door. (If you've ever had to travel for mile after winding mile along a single-track West Highland road, unable to get past a lorry with fish bree pouring out on to the road as it rounds every corner then you'll know all about this distinctive odour).

Finnan haddies were smoked haddocks and kippers were smoked herrings. At some seaside kippering yard the silvery herrings had been taken and hung on a rack above smouldering sawdust. Out of the smoke and tarry black interior of the kiln they emerged with a new look and a new name. The thing about these flat, reddish-golden kippers that really fascinated me was the positioning of their eyes. While herrings' eyes sat conventionally on either side of their heads, in their kipper reincarnation both eyes contrived to stare upwards. It was all to do with the fact that the herrings were split along the middle and then opened out for smoking. Years later, when I saw some celestial goldfish with their two eyes staring heavenwards in a pool at a Buddhist temple in Japan, I thought, somewhat irreverently, of those cross-eyed kippers of my childhood.

But things with fins and gills weren't the only harvest of the deep that filled the fish man's van. Depending on the time of year, he carried a collection of partans in varying sizes, some with huge reddish shells and enormous, shiny black claws that I regarded with no little apprehension. These impressive crab claws could have given small fingers a mighty nip, had the crustacean owner still been living. Despite the fish man's oft-repeated invitation to put my hand out and take hold of one, I never liked to take the chance in case there might be some sudden, miraculous return to life. He laughed every time I shied off from touching the powerful claws that he thrust in my direction and I expect he used the same trick to frighten people my size the length of his round. In a corner of the van, again depending on the season, was sometimes a small heap of glistening seaweed. This dilse was a reddish-green weed gathered along the seashore in the days before eating anything gathered along the shore didn't become such a good idea. My granny swore by it, reckoning that it had health-giving properties. She was evidently ahead of her time; the value of seaweed in the diet is much extolled these days. The thing about all these items is that I recall them as ordinary, everyday foodstuffs. Today, they've been re-branded as 'seafood;' gourmet items 'discovered' by the best restaurants and given some fancy treatment. Whoever would have thought that the once low-cost, Cinderella buckies and the like in the back of the fish man's van would appear much later at the ball, masquerading as expensive *fruits de mer*?

We must also have been a carnivorous lot, to judge by the fact that several butchers served the community. The signs outside their shops announced their dual role as 'Butchers and Poulterers'. Inside their premises, big sides of meat were hacked up on a big wooden slab worn down by years of attack from lethal looking cleavers and fearsome flensing knives. Wifies in the shop weren't afraid to lean over and point to the exact bit they wanted while the butcher was hacking away, making me wonder if any of them ever lost a digit or two in the course of a visit for their meat. Neither were they prepared to leave the premises with any old minced up bit of old cow, watching like hawks as the butcher took a bit of meat, forced it down the funnelled top of the heavy metal mincer and turned a handle till it had been reduced to a little pile of pink, worm-like pieces. Heaven help him if he attempted to insert a bit of meat that had too much fat attached.

Skinned carcases of sheep and pigs with their heads still attached, hung from huge steel hooks. If there was a long queue in the shop, I managed to pass the time agreeably by taking a close look at the bristly snouts of the pigs and the curled horns on the sheep. The copious amounts of blood dripping down were absorbed by handfuls of sawdust. Like a Shinto priest throwing salt over the sumo wrestlers' ring, the butcher liberally scattered handfuls of sawdust over the floor in his own morning ritual. (I was to discover later in student days that the rougher pubs in Aberdeen had an identical floor covering for the same blood absorbing purpose, especially on a Saturday night). The combined smell of raw meat, congealed blood and sawdust in the butchers' shops gave them a distinctive odour that assailed your nostrils before you even set foot in the door.

It was sometimes the practice to have the mounted head of a bull or cow stuck up on the wall as a sort of decoration or perhaps a symbol of the trade, much as the droggist had his gold coloured mortar and pestle above his shop front and the barber had his red and white pole sticking outside. In one butcher's, the accumulated sawdust-derived stue of years crowned the head of a particularly impressive black Highland cow with handlebar horns that wouldn't have disgraced a Spanish bullring, although the vision of a hairy Hielan coo alongside a smoothly immaculate matador in shiny silk breeks may require some leap of imagination. It looked none too pleased at the indignity of its end, glaring down at the stream of customers with nostrils flared in a way you might imagine blowing out angry snorts of steam at Desperate Dan in the Dandy. I never cared for the look of that one; the cold glass eyes seemed to fix on you no matter where you were standing in the shop.

Cut meat was generally laid out in the butcher's window in flat metal trays with bits of green parsley added along the edges for decoration. Shiny white enamel labels bearing such inscriptions as 'Choice,' 'Finest,' or 'Prime Cut,' were stuck like little flags into whatever happened to occupy the trays. Nobody worried too much that meat might be lying about in the open in a sunny shop window and one day I saw something that would be the stuff of a modern health and hygiene inspector's nightmare. In the butcher's window, and in full view of the passing street, though evidently not of the butcher inside, reposed the hairy black and white shop cat, stretched out in the sunshine over a tray of 'Finest' steak mince, basking contentedly on its soft meaty bed.

Our menu at home never rose to the more expensive 'Choice' steaks. More commonly, I was dispatched to fetch a bit of beef for boiling in the big black broth pot, along with what is now fashionably termed 'root vegetables' but we just called them carrots and neeps. Clinging to the bone in the middle, the meat imparted a beefy flavour to ultra-thick soup that lasted for days. For Sunday dinner, the meat and bone were dredged up from the depths of the simmering broth, placed in the centre of an old blue and white willow pattern ashet and surrounded by the orange and yellow lumps of the well cooked vegetables. It would have been no use asking my granny for her broth recipe as her time-honoured way of preparing it consisted of adding a "hanfae o this" and a "suppie o that." No proprietary broth mix was in use. This ad hoc addition of ingredients was fraught with danger.

If she was distracted and the handful of barley happened to be on the over-generous side, wind of the intestinal variety could be an undesirable consequence. Sometimes the big dried peas failed to swell in the cooking and stayed as hard as bullets. A large, matching soup tureen with a lid sat on the old wooden dresser beside a slightly chipped china figure of 'Highland Mary' but was seldom in use for its intended purpose. If a special enough visitor came, it could be quickly emptied of the keys and other items that were deposited for handiness inside, given a quick rinse and filled with steaming broth.

There were no scruples in eating bits and pieces that don't appeal to the modern taste. Sweetbreads, kidney, heart, tongue and tail were all in demand. In their own form of alchemy, the butchers turned head meat into tasty potted heid, set as a pale brown jelly into little wax-coated cardboard containers. Along with new tatties freshly lifted from the garden and some chopped syes or chives, potted heid was a real delicacy. When the warmth of a pale yellow Duke of York tattie gently melted the jelly, it was gourmet eating indeed. I was sent one day to the butcher and had to queue behind a woman who'd come in to ask for some liver. Wiping his hands on a blood-stained apron, the young butcher behind the counter shook his head. Obviously the same situation must have arisen before, because the thwarted customer said, loudly, and in a tone of exasperation, "Hiv ye nivver **ivver** liver?" To tell the truth, I was never too keen on being sent to the butcher's because my granny's parting words before I left the house were invariably something like "Noo, see an tell that butcher mannie that a'm nae sikkin a lot o fat in the mince!" No way was I, a mere wee loon going to look up to a butcher with a big meat cleaver in his hand and tell him that! I'd rather face my granny's black looks and mutterings at home when the fat slowly rose to the surface as the mince simmered away in the brookie pan by the fire.

Chapter 9: Dicing with death

How I was never blown to kingdom come I'll never know. I shudder to think how the tender young shoot of my life might have been nipped in the bud, and it was all to do with the product of our local gasworks. One of the more miss-able attractions of the place, it was dominated by a black mountain of coal awaiting combustion to convert it into gas. For generations, the gasworks had provided a vital energy supply but times had moved on. Now that electricity had come to take its place, it was only rundown properties like ours, where landlords were putting off the evil hour of paying for costly conversion, which still depended on gas supplied through old lead pipes.

There are some olfactory experiences that you just don't forget in this life and the nauseous smell of coal gas is one of them. There was invariably a stale, background whiff of the stuff as soon as you came into our house but you got used to it and didn't really notice after a while. The worn fittings on the gas pipes were probably none too tight and there was always a slight delay between turning on the supply for the light or the cooking ring and getting things lit. Meanwhile, the tap was in the open position, allowing the ill-smelling gas to hiss its merry way to freedom and mingle with the air with which we filled our lungs. The single gas light in the main room was our sole fixed form of illumination in the entire house. The light itself, consisting of a white mantle inside a small translucent glass shade, was attached to the end of a bracket that could be swivelled out from the wall above the fire to spread the light more into the room. As granny turned the brass tap and the gas came hissing out, a satisfying pop occurred the instant it ignited. This was followed by an incandescence that spread gradually through the whole mantle. Gas lighting was far from silent and cast a sickly-looking glow over the proceedings at night-time, an effect unlike anything produced by an electric light bulb. In the interests of economy, the gas was never lit in our house until virtually all vestiges of daylight had gone and my granny pronounced "Weel,weel. We can pit the licht up noo." Besides, her good-going fires threw out enough light to be getting on with basic tasks till the hoolets started their hooting outside and it really was time to put a flame to the mantle.

To light the mantle meant my granny reaching up with a flaming taper in one hand, the other hand ready to turn on the gas. It never entered my head then that we might be dicing with death. After all, you see graphic television images these days of houses reduced to rubble by a catastrophic blast caused by a gas leak. Maybe the whistling draughts, which were one of the least endearing features of our house, dissipated the escaping fumes and spared us any explosion. For the purposes of lighting the mantle, you could buy white wax tapers at the grocer's. These looked like long, severely emaciated candles. You could also purchase red and green slivers of wood called spills but, with economy a byword at home, we usually made our own. From time to time, I was set the task of tearing strips out of a newspaper and tightly folding and refolding them into long concertinas that finally made a tight spill that could be lit from the open fire. A box of spunks, whether Bluebell or Swan Vestas, wasn't of much use since the contents were much too short and burned down quickly.

As time went on, the mantle became so fragile with burning that the slightest touch was enough to cause it to disintegrate in a cloud of fine powder that drifted airily down towards the floor. The trouble was that coming into contact with the thing was hard to avoid if the folded paper started to open and suddenly flared up. More than once, I saw granny put the kibosh on a mantle when her hand jerked as the flame threatened to lick round her fingers. The fact was that mantles had a limited life span and, after hours of intense burning, were just waiting to disintegrate at the slightest excuse. If the last mantle in the house did decide to collapse into powder and there was no spare to hand, it was time to fetch out the Tilley lamp. The brass Tilley had a protruding knob at the base that had to be pushed vigorously in and out to build up pressure and this had to be maintained every so often by another vigorous bout of pumping. Before lighting, you needed to clip on an attachment just below its mantle. This resided alongside the Tilley in its own jar of violet coloured methylated spirit which came in a blue bottle with the warning **POISON – Not to be taken** printed in red on the label. Applying a match caused the spirit to burn with a blue flame before the mantle started to glow. The Tilley also gave out a bright incandescent light and hissed even more loudly than the gas. No matter whether it came from the gas light or the Tilley lamp, the illumination of our house was far from silent. Neighbours who'd undergone a conversion to electricity and seen the new light couldn't believe how quiet their lives had become.

Most culinary activity in the house was centred on the double gas ring with its rubber supply pipe. The ring was used for boiling tatties and vegetables and for cooking mince or stew. We didn't consume a wide range of vegetables. Home grown cabbage was a staple and so was kail. Nutritionists these days extol the value of the vitamin and iron intake that you get from these *brassicas* but I suspect they didn't have in mind the kind of treatment the leaves received on my granny's gas ring where they were boiled till they surrendered all vestige of crispness. The green curly kail was served with a generous dollop of butter on top. Over-boiled carrots were never my favourite vegetable but I was constantly being urged to eat them up so that I would see better in the dark, though I can't say I noticed any difference. New tatties were a much anticipated delicacy of early summer, served whole with butter and finely chopped green leaves of syes which grew in profusion in purple-flowering clumps in just about everybody's garden.

Old tatties were invariably chappit, that's to say they were boiled then pulverised after the addition of a drop of creamy milk. The instrument that my granny wielded with vigour for this purpose was a heavy wooden tattie chapper, or beetle. Sometimes we had a big dollop of chappit tatties with chopped up syes on one of the willow pattern plates as a main course. Another much used wooden implement was the spurkle which was used to stir the heavily salted oatmeal porridge we had for breakfast. The creamy milk for our porridge was always served in a separate bowl. Sometimes we had brose which was oatmeal mixed up with boiling water and a knob of butter. The first time I ever tasted, or even set eyes on, baked beans came as a complete surprise and the reason I remember it so well is that my granny served them unheated and straight out of the tin one cold morning for breakfast. This surprise innovation was obviously meant as a treat but whoever it was that told her about the novelty had obviously not thought to say that the beans would be the better of being heated up, especially at the start of a chilly winter's day.

Small farms in the district kept a house cow for their own family needs and any of the surplus creamy milk was turned into butter and sold or bartered locally. Farm wives made fresh butter with much tedious turning of a handle in kirns. The protracted churning was well worth the effort for the delicious pale butter that resulted. If you had to pick out the odd hair from Flossie or Jess, or whoever had provided the milk in the first place, it was a small price to pay for such a delicacy. Deposited on top of a heap of steaming kail, or thickly clarted over a home-made oatcake, fresh farm butter was a real treat. In this hygiene conscious age, however, I hardly dare mention that a thumb wasn't unknown as the means of spreading it.

Oatcakes were standard fare in our diet. Made from oatmeal, salt and rendered down animal fat, they were flattened out on my granny's solid baking board with a heavy wooden rolling pin before being cut into triangular shapes of broadly similar dimensions. They had to be really carefully handled as they shared with the mantles an over eager tendency to disintegrate. The thin triangles were set up to toast gently in the heat radiating from the open fire. They were referred to as breid, an indication that oatmeal, not wheat flour, was the old standard in our northern parts. It was always a temptation to nibble the uneven edges first as they were toasted dark brown and had a delicious nutty taste. Sometimes I was given the task of toasting a slice of not so fresh loaf at the fire with the aid of a long brass toasting fork with a thistle on the end. Should the bread drop off but happen to land in the hot ash of a quiescent fire, all was not lost; I just quickly retrieved it with the fork, dusted off the grey deposit and continued as if nothing had happened.

*****

A good going fire provided one of my granny's greatest pleasures in life. There was something in the way she regarded fire and hearth that had come down to her from earlier times when the two were the focus of family living. The trouble was she was never content unless the lows were leaping right up the lum. A poor fire was an abomination in her sight. She would come in tut-tutting if she'd been out visiting some neighbour wife with a struggling fire. "I'd a grand cup o tea," she'd say, "bit ye ken, her fire wis near black oot." She was a master of the art

70

of creating a cheery fire, of that there was no doubt. In the winter nights, as she sat back contentedly in her easy chair, looking for pictures in the leaping flames, there was a bit of added interest when some trapped gas suddenly ignited in a lump of coal and made a singing noise. "Harken tae the birdie!" she'd say, appreciating this bit of free entertainment. There were certain house rules regarding the fire that were to be observed on pain of a diatribe on flouting them. On no account was it to be disturbed if all was going well. It was regarded as nothing short of an act of wilful destruction if some unsanctioned hand wielded the poker since it might result in the burning coals collapsing, causing the heart to go out of the fire. In the morning, things were still hot in the grate and the smell of warm ashes permeated the lobby when I was given the task of removing them in a shovel to the grey zinc ais bucket that stood beside the back door.

In the same way that granny detested the sight of an inadequate fire in a neighbour's grate, to have a poorly drawing fire when somebody came to our house was nothing less than a source of shame. If the blame could be laid on weet coal that had been delivered by the coalman and his flatulent steed, his ears would have been burning more than the fire as he got his character in no uncertain way. If all else failed, granny's usual recourse to "a drappie paraffine" (she always said it as if there was 'e' on the end) had the thing bursting into spectacular flame in spite of the wet state of the coal. Not surprisingly, there was a risk inherent in such lively fires, especially when highly flammable paraffin was involved. If the flames started shooting high up the lum, the soot sometimes caught fire and then the lining would start to make ominous cracking noises in the intense heat. At this point, even a seasoned fire stoker like my granny began to get alarmed and I could detect an element of panic creeping in. When she rushed over to the sink, filled a jug of water and threw it on to the flames, I could see that things were getting serious. The splash of water fairly dampened the lows but the side effect was a hissing blast of ash and steam that came out into the room, so this action was to be avoided except *in extremis*. The other response was to fetch down the big blue and silver Cerebos Salt tin that sat on the nearby shelf, and apply a fistful to the offending flames. I loved when this happened. The effect was dramatic and a total delight when the salt released a kaleidoscope of colours. No sooner were things dampened down than granny was looking for the coal shuffel to give the fire another bit of stoking. I knew then that normal service had been resumed.

Getting the fire going in the first place involved the use of a few dry kinlers and some small lumps of coal set carefully on top. If the wood was slightly resinous, so much the better, as quick combustion was assured. However, if a softwood log was heavily impregnated with roset there was some concern as the thing burst too vigorously into flame. The worst culprits in this regard were rosety reets which were bits of pine roots that were hard and so resinous that they sent fiery sparks out on to lino that was already pock-marked from dozens of past flying embers. The sweet smell of freshly chopped kinlers permeated the dusty coal shed, wafting around the heap of coal in whatever state of wetness it reposed.

Another fireplace ritual that was performed occasionally and much to my delight was solely for entertainment. A neighbour, who dropped in from time to time, was adept at it. He'd call for a brown paper pyock, such as loose sugar came in from the grocer's, then open it, turn it upside down and tweak up the two bottom corners like sticking up lugs. Thus prepared for lift-off, it was placed, upside down, inside the heavy metal fender as close as possible to the fire. If the two ears were lit almost simultaneously, the thing ascended slowly in the manner of a hot air balloon, the up-draught lifting it straight out of sight up the chimney. The trick was to ensure as even as possible a lighting of the two lugs. Any uneven burning created a difficulty with lift-off that was as hazardous as the malfunction of a space rocket, causing the thing to burst into flames and come back down to earth again before it had hardly started its ascent. Naturally, this was much to the alarm of anybody sitting close by the fire when flaming fragments descended round about their feet and they had to make a quick shift. In fact, a great deal of sitting close to fires took place, especially on long winter evenings, as was all too obvious on the legs of some female shoppers when you saw them out for their earans in the morning. Over-proximity to the open flames caused their skin to become birsled, creating a marbled pattern that was as much a feature of the winter season as the Jack Frost patterns on the inside of my bedroom window panes.

Chapter 10: Wirds

My granny had a way with words (wirds, she'd have said), and her native Doric provided her with a rich miscellany of sayings and expressions. She came of an older generation and her everyday speech was laced with words and pronunciations that were already falling into disuse. Perhaps that wasn't so surprising, since changes in post-war life included the things folk said and the way that they said them. Outside influences, not least the wireless and the world of the picters, were bringing in new words, and their advent could be quite rapid. Younger housewives in aprons and turbans were suddenly going about their morning dusting, singing American melodies like the 1950 hit:

"Put another nickel in.

In the nickelodeon.

All I want is lovin' you

And music! music! music!"

I didn't have any notion what a nickelodeon might be – and possibly neither did they.

Even at home, old words were starting to disappear. The knock (with the *k* pronounced at the beginning) was what my granny called the wood-encased monstrosity of a thing that sat on the over-heated mantelpiece above her roaring coal fires. I learned to tell the time on it, referring to its two ornate black hands. It was an ugly looking object and I hated its depressing, slow tick. Its poor relation was a small, modern clock with an alarm, referred to as the knockie, to distinguish it from its larger relation. The use of the diminutive was very common and 'ie' was added to the end of all sorts of things as a matter of course, like quinie, loonie, doggie, cattie. If the neighbour's cat looked suspiciously large, granny would mutter "Ah doot that cattie's awa tae kittle." Sure enough, in due time the union of cattie and the opportunist tom cat that had seduced her during one of her nocturnal outings would be blessed with a litter of kittlins.

When my granny spoke about anything the evening before, estreen was the word she used. If a stormy night had rattled the roof slates she'd report next morning "It wis gey coorse estreen. Ah thocht the reef wis near gyaun tae cam aff the hoose." If it wasn't your fault she'd say "It wisna yer wyte." If I was told to go and ask a neighbour about something, it would be "Gyang an spier at her." Something considered a bit old fashioned was aul farrant; a wretch was a vratch, and a person didn't work but vrocht.

Some of the plurals and collective nouns which we used at home sounded quite different from the English. The cattle that grazed in the surrounding parks were kye or nowt. If you had one shoe it was ae shee and when you had a pair you possessed twa sheen. Two eyes were twa een, and if I should happen to complain to my granny that I had an eye irritation, I might be asked "Is't jist the ae ee that ails ye?" If the inflammation persisted in the same eye, the question could be "Is't aye the **ae** ee?" where aye, pronounced more like ey, meant 'still.' It was a mortal sin in school to answer the teacher with the affirmative "Aye" when the English 'yes' was the only acceptable reply. There was also the word's double employment in "Aye, aye!" which was the brief greeting used when passing somebody in the street, sometimes in its alternative form "Aye, min!" if the person you met happened to be male. The state of the weather became the greeting of the moment. Somebody passing you on a warm and sunny day would nod and say "It's a rael bonny day!" The converse, in times of wind and driving rain, was a grudging "Coorse day!" where even the definite article was dropped in the hurry to get past with head down and coat collar pulled up. The terse "Aye is't!" reply would barely be heard against the wind as the person moved rapidly by.

The phrase "Michty aye!" signified emphatic agreement. The use of "Michty!" on its own was more an expression of surprise, doubtless an innocuous contraction of the more blasphemous "God Almichty!" which was used for purposes of extreme emphasis. When words failed her in situations of anger or even exasperation, my granny was given to shaking her fist, only at home it was her niv. Her hair was held in a bun at the back with a long preen. Had you been of a poetic disposition, you would have no shortage of words to rhyme with preen. You could look up into the night sky and see the meen; in the morning your porridge was suppit wi a speen, and after Sunday's denner the neighbour's dog was presented with the been. You could make a splash in the water by throwing in a steen, go out in the company of a freen, or just go on your own, yer leen. Above was abeen and when things were finished, they were a deen.

The use of the double negative added an interesting touch. If I was sent to look in the press for a box of matches and found that there weren't any left, I'd report back "There's nae neen." Something that was totally useless was "nae eese tae naebody." This linguistic turn was well illustrated when I recently heard a North-east voice utter the sage words: "There's nae naethin that naebody canna dee." Another distinctive part of our speech was the way words ended. The past tense of verbs generally involved the use of '-it' at the end. For example, when it was time to harvest our tatties they weren't dug up but liftit; things that were cut were cuttit; when something was knocked over it was coupit; something that hurt hurtit, and if you belched you riftit.

In wet weather, if you got mud all over your boots they were said to be clartit wi dubs. I was amused to note once a reference to a government minister called Lord Dubs. Had his remit been in Scottish agricultural matters, I could just imagine the pithy comments of North-east farmers. Playing with muddy deposits was always a temptation when we were very little. The wettest variety we knew as sappy dubs on account of their consistency. After very heavy rain I was forbidden to go to certain places on the grounds that they were ower dubby. Should you want to denote a strong degree of adherence, you employed the word clarty.

There were particular words for amounts and one of them was curn. Somebody who died and left a few thousand pounds was said to have left a curn thoosans. Small amounts were a puckle, or a pucklie if it was an even smaller quantity. A suppie was an entirely undefined amount, though everybody knew what it meant in relation to the circumstances, and could involve anything from sugar to paraffin. Twa-three also meant a small amount, said as if the last e was missing. When she was ready to start the fire, my granny would say to me "Awa an fess ben twa-three kinlers."

When it came to the matter of clothing, semmits were what we called vests and sarks were shirts. On washing days (invariably the same day of the week) examples of these garments often shared our neighbour's outside washing line with a couple of pairs of his white lang draaers, garments that kept him warm in winter inside thick breeks that were held up by galluses. From time to time, his washin tow revealed to the world his skin-clinging combies, something much favoured by old mannies where semmit and draaers were combined in practical harmony to repulse the draughts.

When it came to headgear, berets in khaki, black or navy blue were much in vogue. Pulled down to one side, they were favoured by men going to their work, often on a heavy black push bike equipped with a dynamo light for the dark winter days. The womenfolk's tammie equivalent lacked the narrow band of leather of the service headgear, came in a wider range of colours and was worn in as fashionable a way as they could manage. There seemed to be so many ex-service berets around that you wonder if somebody had made a monumental error of over-ordering in the headgear department at the War Ministry. After their contribution to the defence of the nation, berets often ended up in a less glorious role: as a covering for a bike seat, making an otherwise hard leather saddle just a bit more comfortable on the doup. If you didn't get hold of one brought back from service days, there were Army Surplus stores in Aberdeen that, despite their name, sold redundant items from all three of the services at low cost. When I was at university and wanting to purchase my first sleeping bag for a camping trip, I was examining some ex-army examples in the window of one of the stores when my eyes lit on a notice that said "Ex-WRAF KNICKERS" and then, as an afterthought in brackets, "Outsize." It entered my imagination that, with the ends of the legs tied, the voluminous undergarments in the window might have doubled as emergency parachutes.

A favourite word of my granny's in connection with what I wore was blad, uttered, for example, in the warning before I was allowed outside the house with new footwear: "Dinna blad yer gweed sheen!" If I failed to heed the admonition and returned to the house with the new black leather all scuffed, I could expect the none too pleased response "Ye vratch, ye've geen an bladdit yer new sheen!" We were much more happit up in winter clothes than many schoolchildren seem to be today when fashion appears to have run ahead of practicality and health considerations, and loons wander about in thin tee-shirts and quines in skirts so short that they could be mistaken for curtain pelmets.

Mind you, in the primary school, and even into secondary, our knees were well exposed to the elements. Our short grey breeks had button-up spavers at the front that were a job to cope with when fingers were really cold and numb on winter days. The accompanying knee length socks were held up by black elastic garters and when your legs got wet on the way to school on a coorse winter morning they became red and fired with all the rubbing against the bottom edges of your shorts and along the tops of your wellies. Going off to school in winter weather meant wrapping up in several layers and it could get very warm when you got into class. This could result in itching in the vicinity of the armpits, a condition known as yokie oxters. The trouble was that relief wasn't always easy to come by. The teacher didn't like to see any hand go up a jersey to assuage the itching, as she had a particular distaste of the practice of scratching.

When a whole lot of us with sypin weet claes came into the classroom, a bit of a yoam tended to rise as the heat drew out moisture from clothes that were probably washed a bit less often than is the case in today's society with its ubiquitous washing machines, washing powders and endless supplies of hot water. At home, water was boiled in a big kettle at the fire. Shirt collars that were fule were treated to a big square cake of yellow Sunlight washing soap and rubbed vigorously up and down on the corrugated side of a washing board, a household item that was later to find unexpected stardom as a backing instrument in skiffle groups.

Expressions to do with money, especially concerning any perceived parsimony, were amusing in their own way. Lashin oot was the phrase used when somebody decided to spend in an unexpected sort of way. Lettin the win in amang yer siller meant parting with money for some purpose. (Bawbees could be substituted here for siller). Much more was implied in the comment "She's lettin the mochs oot o her purse," for that suggested that the purse was so infrequently opened that the insects might have taken up residence like they did in unopened clothes drawers. In the currency of the time, ten bob notes were worth a lot of money. Lower down the scale came half-croons, florins, shillins (bobs), saxpences (tanners), echt-sided threepenny bits, maiks or ha'pennies and even farthins which I especially liked as they had a picture of a wren on one side.

"Yon chiel's as feel as a maik watch" was a devastating comment on some lad's intelligence, or rather lack of it. Some things in the language wouldn't go down too well in today's politically correct world, but to be described as feel wasn't exactly unkind. It was used in "Awa an nae be feel!" where it just meant being mildly stupid. Gowk, the word for a cuckoo, sometimes substituted for feel, as in "Ye daft gowk!" Gypit was used to describe a state of immature silliness, while glaikit implied something more permanent and maybe hereditary; that's to say a family might have more than one glaikit individual in its midst. When some lassies transgressed over the boundaries of quiet, conventional behaviour, folk said "Yon quines is affa hallirackit."

Somebody considered to be a bit perverse was described as contermacious and anyone who took an undue interest in other people's affairs, to the point of noting every coming and going from behind their white screens, was guilty of ull faschiouns. The latter was not to be confused with the verb 'to fash', often employed when you didn't want somebody to be bothered over an issue, when the apposite expression was "Dinna fash yersel." A much used and highly expressive word was dunt. In our house, "Gie't a dunt!" was a common command from my granny to me to get the old radio working again when the sound cut out. Giving the thing a knock on the top with my fist was generally enough to restore connection to the Home Service and keep us in touch with the latest with the McFlannels. More serious was the aftermath of a fall, when some person wasn't the better for having tripped over and banged his head. "Hie's gien himsel a nesty dunt on the heid," was the comment, as if the unfortunate casualty had done it deliberately.

Although I wasn't aware of it at the time, many of our words had come to us from the French, dating back to the days of the Auld Alliance between Scotland and France when we weren't on the best of terms with our Sassenach neighbours. At Sunday dennertime my granny laid out the customary bit of biled beef on her big blue and white ashet (French *assiette*). When the weather was dry, we watered the garden with our much dented, galvanised watering can which we called the rooser (*arosser*, to water) and when darkness fell, we listened to the hoolets (*hulot*, an owl) hooting in the trees outside.

I must confess I didn't give a lot of thought to the language of home. It was just what we spoke and what generations of my North-east forebears had spoken before that. But the passage of time fairly alters your perception of things and these days I've come to value more and more the expressive wirds and sayings of home all those years ago. They went with an unhurried style of life that has passed, replaced by a more frenetic way of doing things and going about our daily living.

People pay a fortune these days to fly thousands of miles away to experience different cultures. Horizons have been opened up in a way that would have been unimaginable in my granny's time, but in an age when people lived out their days in a more sedentary, circumscribed lifestyle, communities were more distinct from one another and differences in speech and even culture could be experienced within a few miles. These days, the barriers imposed by distance have gone due to ease of communication on the ground and through media influence. Increasingly, the stamp of uniformity is applied, not least in the way people speak with inflections derived from the trans-Atlantic and Australian characters in the TV 'soaps'. At the same time, school teachers have become used to seeing the fanciest of celebrity names on their class registers, with Geordies now relegated to endangered breed status.

Chapter 11: Ben the hoose

You could say that our 'facilities' at home had something in common with the Grand Old Duke of York. While his men were neither up nor down, our place was sort of neither in nor out. To reach there, you had to go through our long, dark lobby and out through an inner back door fastened with a metal sneck. At some stage, the old house had been given a bit of an addition for the comfort and (pardon the pun) convenience of the indwellers. Beside this outshot, my granny's enormous mangle with its bleached wooden rollers stood in all its cast iron glory. The arrangement suggested some sort of afterthought of nature; joined to the house yet somehow not exactly part of it. But at least we had the benefit of running water.

Responding to a call of nature in our house was generally referred to as "gyan ben the hoose." If the expression seemed to imply some sort of journey, indeed it was, for it meant traversing the length of the ill-lit lobby to get there. When the place was considered to be in need of a very occasional brighten up, it received an application of whitewash, with the result that the inside walls were covered in countless layers which were constantly peeling away in large flakes. Though a visit didn't involve going outside exactly, the winter winds still managed to come in through the big gap under the door, transforming themselves into moaning and whistling draughts that even the thick, home-made rag mat placed along the bottom was hard pressed to repel. Humble though the surrounds might be, there was, however, a crowning glory to the place; a thing of grandeur that put most other facilities of my acquaintance firmly in the shade. It was the commodious pan that sat there in all its Victorian splendour, a tribute to the grand scale in which such symbols of the might of Empire had been conceived. Attached to the wall above the pan was an equally impressive cast iron cistern with the manufacturing foundry's name in raised letters on the side. To effect a flush, you had to pull on the end of the hanging metal chain whose handle was shaped to accommodate three adult fingers. By dint of pulling the chain down hard and fast (the simultaneous nature of the procedure was an art that had to be mastered if a first time, full-scale flush was to be assured), an impressive cascade was unleashed from the cistern. When properly pulled, the reward was a downfall worthy of Niagara. The maelstrom that followed in the pan had something in common with the Corrievreckan whirlpool, before the water rushed out of sight with a prolonged and satisfying gurgle. To manage more than a disappointing trickle, the trick was to catch the thing unawares and give the chain a sharp, downward pull, or what my granny would have called "a gweed rug doon." You could tell when an inexperienced user was in the house, because you could hear the chain being given repeated and resounding abortive pulls before the cistern grudgingly deigned to open the flood gates and let the water flow out.

For the comfort of its users, the pan was furnished with a most generously proportioned and well polished seat of quality brown mahogany. The tree that had given its all for our convenience (and that of who knows how many who went before) would have grown in a steamy tropical forest in some far flung corner of the Empire, till the loggers moved in with their elephants. As befitted a product of those glory days, the seat had been crafted on a grand scale and certainly wasn't designed with the more modest posteriors of minors in mind. When I was very little, it was the stuff of nightmares to imagine tumbling backwards into the foam, never to be seen again.

Within easy reach of any occupier, a wad of cut-up newspaper squares hung lopsidedly from a length of rough, slightly yellow string and this, in turn, was tied to a six inch nail. As its name might suggest, this binder tow was intended primarily for binding up sheaves of corn and the like on farms but served its non-agricultural purpose eminently well. The reason for the lopsidedness was that after the pieces of newspaper had been cut to roughly the same dimensions, the sharp point of a pair of scissors was used to make a hole for the string in a corner of the sheets. These cut-out squares were naturally a source of interest and enlightenment during any sojourn, albeit that the news they contained might be a little dated (though everybody knows the fascination of old newspapers). When the worn out linoleum had to be lifted off our lobby floor for replacement, the dusty yellowed news underneath was studied by my granny with her big magnifying glass for days, never mind that it was decades out of date, not just a mere month or two. In studying what was printed on the newspaper squares, there was an inevitable element of frustration when your attention was taken by some item of local interest, only to find that half of it must be on another sheet altogether, so you just had to content yourself with an incomplete bit of information and try to make sense of what was left. Sometimes I wonder if my interest in words may have had part of its origin at least in the times spent in this most basic of reading rooms. Some of the civic dignitaries of the district who'd happily posed at the time for press photos would have been none too flattered to know that the newspaper in which they'd featured was now being put to such a basic purpose.

Our place was nothing if not multifunctional. To the roles of convenience and reading room could be added, to my infinite pleasure, that of wildlife refuge. To someone like myself, with a young naturalist's curiosity, the place was a most satisfying sanctuary for all manner of creatures that had moved in from the wild. The four little panes of thick glass on the inward opening window were festooned with wyver webs containing the desiccated body shells of insects that had sought sanctuary inside, only to end up on the resident arachnids' dinner menu. They weren't daft, the spiders, appreciating their dry board and lodgings and occasional food supply. One or two enormous specimens with long legs made their lairs in the dark corners and you could see them scuttling back if you caught them unawares. As soon as autumn temperatures began to fall, the odd tortoiseshell butterfly decided it was time to come in from the outside, fold up its wings and prepare to pass the winter upside down on the roof. At the same time, dark grey slaters marched indoors in their droves, enacting their own little yearly transhumance. For these flat-bodied woodlice that came in from the cold, the place must have appeared warm enough, but that's not the way I viewed it on a chilly winter's night.

To beat the frost, all the exposed pipes leading into the cistern were wrapped round with, or, in our parlance, wuppit roon wi, hairy brown lagging. Even so, my granny dreaded a freeze-up in the exposed lead piping. She was willing to take no chances when late afternoon skies cleared and temperatures began to plummet. Then it was time to do battle with the frost as she moved the round black metal paraffin stove with its three squat legs in from the shed. The aim of the exercise was to ward off any freezing that might burst the pipes, certainly not to provide creature comforts for the users. In the interests of fuel saving, the wick was turned down as low as possible without actually extinguishing the little blue and yellow flame. The manufacturers had provided holes on the top to let the heat out and had thought to introduce a bit of artistry into the matter at the same time. They had not, however, taken into account the sensitivities of such as myself, and the result was definitely not to my liking. The holes came in all sorts of shapes, ranging from diamonds and stars to fancy swirls. During daylight hours there was no problem but in the dark of night the draught made the flame flicker, sending its light up through the top openings and projecting scary patterns on to the whitewashed roof. When weird faces with staring eyes and malevolent, downturned mouths danced across the ceiling and leered down, I was none too keen to linger long.

Given the place's geographical location in terms of the house layout, at the furthest extremity of the lobby, the last thing you wanted was a nocturnal journey with an icy wind whistling past your lugs. Armed with a small paraffin lamp, a winter night's expedition ben the hoose had more than a little in common with setting out on a trek into some dark and chilling Arctic waste. I learned from uncomfortable experience that it was better to go easy on the lemonade before going to bed to avoid putting too much pressure on a still-growing bladder with limited capacity. There were, however, times when nature was wont to take the upper hand. Should the dreaded journey then become both necessary and urgent, there was nothing else for it but to set out into the blackness, flickering flame held out in front. At such moments I envied my friends their more conventional facilities, not to mention the electric light that made them far more user friendly.

Putting up the generous seat revealed some detail that was otherwise largely obscured when the thing was in its default down position. On the back wall of the pan was inscribed the name and address of the firm of 'sanitary potters' who'd created the thing in the first place. I was always amazed that the writing, printed in an appropriate shade of sanitary blue, remained as clear as ever, despite having being subjected to flushes without number in the pan's long career. It also had a kind of royal crest embossed upon it but whether it was 'By appointment' or not, and therefore deemed worthy of accommodating a royal posterior, I'm not sure now. I always thought the name Stoke-on-Trent had a fine sort of ring to it. No place round our way was grand enough to have even one hyphen in its name, let alone two. Years later, on a student field trip to the Potteries of Staffordshire, I was able to see the smoking red brick chimneys and beehive kilns of pottery premises that produced everything from the finest bone china teacups with thin handles you couldn't put your finger through to the lowliest, utility toilet bowls. I felt that I somehow already knew the place when we went into Stoke itself as I'd looked at the name on the pan so often before its blue letters were immersed in the swirling waters. When our bus passed a large sign above the entrance to one pottery, an outburst of student mirth was provoked by the inscription "Jones and Shufflebottom, Sanitary Potters."

Since our house was lacking in any kind of water heating system, all hot water for washing purposes came from an enormous brown enamel kettle that sat beside the ever lit fire. The one tap at the heavy brown earthenware sink below the window in the living room-cum-kitchen supplied only cold water, and that varied in temperature according to the season. A sloosh of icy cold water on your face after you'd just got up on a winter's morning was guaranteed to drive away any lingering urge to get back to bed as the shock to the system was immediate and dramatic.

There was a woeful lack of illumination in the house and my small bedroom had no fixed lighting at all. A paraffin lamp supplied whatever light was needed at bedtime, but there was even a knack in keeping that working properly. Turn up the wick too far and you just succeeded in coating the inside of the narrow glass funnel in a black film of soot. This wasn't a popular thing to do as it meant the glass had to be washed out with hot soapy water and there was always the risk of something happening to the thin glass if it slipped out of my granny's hands when she was lifting it out from the soapy suds in the sink. Depending on the state of the wick, the fumes tended to hang about the room in varying strengths but I didn't mind; I never found a mild dose of paraffin fumes too disagreeable.

My bedroom lacked the comfort of any form of heating though I don't suppose you miss what you've never known. To sleep with one of the black paraffin stoves in the room would have risked bringing in the frightening figures to dance on the roof and, besides, I might have expired in the night through breathing in the noxious fumes. During the coldest winter nights when Jack Frost was busy creating his ferny patterns from my breath on the inside of the glass, the bed was like an ice box with its smooth white cotton sheets. Something close to frost bite was avoided by introducing a bit of warmth between the cold sheets on freezing cold nights. This involved my granny filling a bed warmer with boiling hot water from the kettle. We had two warmers. One was a fairly flat container made of copper with a screw-top lid on the top. It would have taken the skin off the soles of your feet if you'd had it into the bed without the protection of its crocheted woollen cover. Short of putting an old fashioned warming pan filled with red hot coals from the fire between the sheets, it would be difficult to think of a more effective, if skin scorching, bed warmer. The other was a heavy brown and natural coloured stoneware pig with a screw top in the centre that worked on the same principle. I knew from painful experience that if I accidentally pushed my feet down hard against the unyielding earthenware, I'd crack my toes with such force that it would put me off sleeping for ages afterwards. While these things were meant to keep you warm, it has to be said that they didn't necessarily guarantee an undisturbed night's sleep. If the pig made a bid for freedom between the slippery sheets and dropped heavily on to the linoleum-covered floor, the thump was loud enough to arrest my granny's snores from her bed in the living room/kitchen next door, and that took some doing. When the cover was removed from the copper bed warmer, its many dents and bashes spoke volumes about how often it had tumbled on to the floor in the night, and the number of times it must have put paid to somebody's slumbers.

Chapter 12: Visitors from afar

Children think nothing of jetting off to far-flung destinations these days. In fact, some of them would feel decidedly hard done by if they didn't get their yearly fortnight of holiday sun and tan at some Spanish Costa or other. Long distance travel certainly didn't feature in my early years. That's not to say that we didn't come into contact with visitors from afar, but I'll come to them in a moment after I've said something about those who came from not so afar.

There was no shortage of coming and going from our house. In that regard, things were no different from what went on round about where we lived. Visiting was an important form of social contact and a valued part of daily living. Newsin with a neighbour was a pleasurable way to pass the time of day and the means of picking up some fresh bit of news. Looking back on it, I realise how much I was being brought up in a sharing culture. This sharing ranged from everyday claik, in which current local on-goings of note were discussed when two or more female neighbours got together, to the disposal of surplus vegetables in the bountiful days of summer. At the times when home-grown garden produce was plentiful, anything extra was given away; nothing was left to waste or rot. Besides, there was a limit to the amount of rhubarb any one family could comfortably consume. Neighbours popped in at any hour of the day to impart some interesting piece of news, especially if it had a spicy edge to it. In this way, key items of community interest were communicated and broadcast as effectively as if they'd been on local radio. Who in the vicinity was expectin (the word 'pregnant' was never uttered) and whose banns were to be cried in the kirk ahead of their marriage ceremony were items of interest because they concerned individuals known to everybody in our part of the community. As such, they were legitimate subjects for discussion. A wifie who lived close by prided herself on "kennin a the latest." She was quite put out if somebody asked her about some fresh bit of gossip and she had to admit ignorance. "Nivver mind," she'd say, taking a deep breath and rising to the challenge and determined to remedy the situation,"bit ah'll fin oot."

From time to time, visitors called at the house from a different part of town and this naturally added a dash of fresh interest. We had a visit one afternoon from a woman who'd just flitted with her man and bairns out of cramped rented accommodation in a rundown property into the comparative luxury of a Prefab. This word, short for prefabricated, was applied to the box-like housing units rapidly assembled out of sections of grey, corrugated asbestos. You can still see the odd one surviving out in the countryside today, albeit in a dilapidated state. Redundant Prefabs sometimes found a second use on farms as hen houses after they were replaced in due course by more permanent council housing. I imagine the hens would have been as delighted with the standard of their new accommodation as the original tenants had been.

Prefabs formed distinctive, neat little colonies in towns up and down the land in the immediate post-war years as part of a Government initiative to address the acute housing shortage of the time. This pressing state of affairs was exacerbated by the 'baby boom' when servicemen returned after hostilities came to an end and were anxious to make up for lost time. A woman who came to call on my granny one day had been re-housed with her family. Our visitor could hardly contain the excitement of moving into her Prefab home, describing everything about it in interminable detail. You would have thought it was some sprawling stately pile she'd flitted into, not a wee Prefab, she took that long to get through it all. Anyway, after all this, and having consumed a succession of cups of tea, she needed to pay a visit ben the hoose. "My, bit ye've a richt gweed flush," she commented on her return, an undisguised touch of envy in her voice. "Ah like ma new hoose fine," she added, "bit, ye ken, wir flush is nae worth a damn."

A different group of visitors came by from time to time to offer their services. Some called in the hope of selling some item or other and others just appeared on the doorstep to ask for things. A well-dressed woman made regular calls round the doors with a big woven straw basket on her arm. A clean white dish towel spread across the top hid the contents from view and thwarted the attention of any passing flies. I could hardly wait till she laid the basket on the step as I knew that a mouth watering spread of home baking in all shapes and forms would be revealed when she removed the covering. Perhaps she was a widow supplementing a meagre income by baking her iced cakes and delicious jam-filled sponges and selling them round the doors. Whatever the circumstances, she certainly was an accomplished home baker and a welcome caller as far as I was concerned. She definitely didn't come into the category of 'hawkers,' who were regarded by everybody with a bit of suspicion when they appeared, as some of them had a shifty look and you wondered what they might be eyeing up.

There was an old character who really frightened me and I would have done anything for my granny not to let her in when she came chappin at the door. But that wasn't the way of things in our house and hospitality would always be offered to anyone she considered to be in need. "Peer aul craitur," my granny would say as she went to cut off a thick slice of loaf and pour a cup of strong black tea from the ever present big pot beside the fire. But I had a different take on things, especially when I was very small. From her scary appearance, I was convinced our visitor must be a witch. The ends of the faded tartan plaid round her shoulders were pulled together at the front with a giant safety pin. The staring, misty blue eyes and tousled grey hair gave her a wild look and when she laughed the sound came from somewhere in her throat as a strange cackle. The sight of the sole remaining bottom front tooth did nothing to enhance her appearance and I cowered into a corner. I didn't care for her occasional visits at all and was only too pleased when she went off again having loudly slurped her tea and tackled the tough crusts with the aid of the one tooth. "Fit's that smell?" I asked as she left after one of her visits. My granny put her finger to her lips. "Meths!" she whispered. I thought of the glass jar in which we kept the mauve coloured methylated spirits for starting our Tilley lamp and wondered how on earth anyone could possibly consume the queer smelling stuff.

Much more welcome than the opportunist hawkers were the amiable families of travelling folk that had been coming round the district for years. When the fine days took them and their carts on to the open road again, their little humpies sometimes sprung up like toadstools on the edges of woods outside the town. These easily dismantled homes were no more than lengths of faded canvas stretched over a framework of pliable saplings. From the outside they looked far too small to accommodate big families. To judge by the squads of bairns playing around, the fecundity of the parents was never in any doubt. As they travelled around the countryside, they carried on their metal working skills, willing to turn their hand to bits and pieces of repair, like patching the bottom of a much used pail. Some of the women went round the doors with baskets of home-made clothes pegs made out of thin branches which had been cut from the trees around their camping places. They appeared, along with the swallows, as the days got steadily longer and the weather took a turn for the better. And, just like the same birds, they disappeared as suddenly when the days started to draw in. I knew from our teacher that the swallows flew off to Africa when the colder weather came but I never knew where these summer visitors wintered. They just took to the road again and vanished out of our lives for another year.

Another seasonal visitor who worked in metal but in an entirely different way was an old mannie who turned up in the summer time carrying a small portable knife grinder. He wore a green tweed jacket that must have graced a more affluent back in its better days but it was now quite gone at the cuffs and elbows and had become well polished round the pockets. The bonnet that had once been a match for the jacket was now so worn and greasy that parts of it shone in the sunshine. Although knives were generally sharpened by my granny at home, using the front doorstep as a makeshift whetstone, some folk had their own grinders consisting of a circular piece of heavy stone mounted on a wooden frame. As the handle was turned, you placed the blade against the spinning stone till it took on a fresh edge. We didn't possess such a thing, however, and it was here that our visitor's services came in. He worked to a well practised routine. Step one was to settle himself down on the front doorstep and lay out the various blades requiring his attention. The next bit was the one I enjoyed the most. Once he was ready to begin, he removed his bonnet and placed it, upside down, by his side on the step. At this point he revealed an almost completely baldie heid that was even more shiny on top than the bonnet that covered it. But now came the *piece de resistance* of the whole show, when he put his none too clean fingers into his mouth and deftly extricated his false teeth. I was fascinated by the long, glistening strands of adhering saliva that were casually brushed away on his worn cuff, as if they were no more than gossamer, and the pink and white dentures were placed carefully on the bonnet. Whether he couldn't concentrate so well when he had them in or whether he was just scared they'd drop out as he worked, I wasn't quite sure, but the set of teeth sat beside him through the entire process, grinning inanely to themselves. Interesting though it was to watch our knife sharpener at work, I couldn't keep my eyes off the companion presence on the step. The sharpening over, the teeth were given a quick wipe against his jacket to remove any adhering dirt and popped back in to their rightful place. He then put his bonnet back on, collected his shilling or whatever the payment, and away he went. The knife sharpening was a useful, low cost service and the entertainment incurred no extra charge.

Once a year, striking black and white figures made a brief appearance round the doors. Nuns in long black habits and shiny white coifs from some distant convent came round to solicit donations for their charitable works. Against their habits, their faces seemed really pale, as if they didn't see the light of day too often. I was reluctant to open the door to such alien beings. One, who had a thin, beak-like nose with round wire-framed spectacles balanced on top, reminded me of a bird. More specifically, she put me in mind of an owl. I'd never actually been face to face with one of the birds but I thought she resembled the picture of a brown owl that the teacher had pinned up above the nature table in class. Ours wasn't a household of the nuns' particular religious persuasion, but it was just my granny's way to give a donation of some kind, even though it might be just be a sixpence.

*****

Gardening for the pot took priority over the growing of flowers in most back yairds and those who grew vegetables generally cultivated a row or two of onions, or ingins in the local parlance. Sometimes there could be problems with insect attack or just with getting them to dry in mochie autumn weather, so the arrival of a source of big glossy onions could be quite timely. The Ingin Johnnies who came round the doors on big black push bikes, brought well-polished onions with their dry yellow stems beautifully plaited into tresses that were draped over the handlebars. They spoke in a way that I found hard to understand, which wasn't very surprising, since they had limited English, and what they did have was mixed with words from their own Celtic tongue, since they came all the way from Brittany. The tresses were themselves a work of art, holding together fine looking onions that had rubbed shoulders with artichokes in the fields in that northern part of France. Of course, it would have been a complete waste of time bringing artichokes round our doors, as tastes were decidedly conservative and anything as foreign sounding would be guaranteed to meet with no demand whatsoever. But the ingins; now that was a different matter, and the arrival of the Ingin Johnnies was a real event, something to bring a brief bit of colour into our lives. When they appeared in the district there was no doubting that foreigners had arrived in our midst. Some of them sported impressive Continental moustaches and, like the stereotypical Frenchman, they wore flat black berets.

If the Ingin Johnnies with their moustaches and berets brought a breath of foreign parts, the swarthy, bearded Sikh gentlemen with their turbans were even more interesting as far as the neighbourhood youngsters were concerned. I watched, fascinated, as they lugged their heavy brown leather cases around, often one in each hand. "Ah dinna ken fit wye that mannie's airms are nae pullt oot o jint," observed my granny as one of these travellers from the east was spotted coming round the doors with two immense, heavily laden cases that he could barely lift. These men were greeted with a real welcome as the bulging cases were a treasure chest of clothing and the contents were more reasonably priced than in the shops. Semmits, nicht goons and knickers were laid out on doorsteps for inspection, with a charming smile from the pedlars and red-faced embarrassment from their potential customers as an array of the most intimate forms of ladies' apparel was exposed to public view. Generally speaking, the womenfolk didn't have the confidence to invite such exotic looking strangers in over the step but were charmed by the compliments and smiles they received. A little bit of charm and flattery was all part of the sales process, encouraging an initially reluctant customer to open up her purse and part with her siller. When I learned that these enterprising salesmen came all the way from India, a splodge of empirical pink on our teacher's shiny classroom wall map, I was mightily impressed. India...Now that **was** afar!

"Bliddy spurgies!"

The familiar voice of our elderly neighbour sounded none too pleased. My young ears pricked up in expectation of a further volley of swearing to come. From experience, I knew that, as sure as summer follows spring, there would be more of the same to follow. His command of the more colourful aspects of language had earned him something of a reputation locally. "That mannie fairly kens the wye tae sweer," my granny was wont to say, shaking her head, pursing her lips and giving a disapproving tut each time he employed his colourful vocabulary in my hearing. I knew that the outflow, once started, wouldn't be easily stemmed and I waited with anticipation. In the matter of adjectives, "bliddy" was by far his favourite, prefacing just about every noun that he used. When someone told him something of which he disapproved, he would inevitably pause for a moment then add "Ach, that's nae bliddy eese ava." Had the Guinness Book of Records been around in those days, he'd certainly have been a prime contender for the world record for the greatest use of the word in one sentence.

Something had clearly riled him, and the measure of his ire became even more apparent as he approached our open back door. I went to see what was happening. Finding that he now had an audience, he unleashed a fresh volley of vituperation. This was accompanied by the spray of warm spittle that descended on my bare knee. I thought of his stale, tobacco-smelling breath and his regular voiding of throaty phlegm and could have wished at that moment that my short grey breeks weren't quite so short. I pulled down the end of my jersey sleeve and brushed my leg to rid it of the offending matter, eager to find out what had happened. Naturally, I was delighted by the colourful nature of his continuing diatribe. Out of his well filled cornucopia of curses, swears and sundry other imprecations flowed a steady stream that was a delight to the ears of a child old enough to appreciate the impropriety of it.

Whatever the cause of the provocation, it was obvious that the local sparrows had somehow been involved, though for reasons as yet unclear. Standing at our door in his customary garden garb of worn cloth cap, faded blue dungarees and black wellies with slightly frayed turn-downs, he continued to hiss his indignation through a mass of wiry grey moustache hairs that sprouted in no consensus of direction and which largely masked both lips. This impressively unmanaged growth was one of the wonders of my childhood, not least on account of its orange tint which was at its most intense in the middle, fading gradually to either side. The colouring, more accurately the discolouring, resulted from the moustache's dual role as facial decoration and filter to the blue tobacco reek that ascended, incense-like, from an ever-present, smouldering cigarette. Even at the height of his fulminations, it clung on resolutely to a hidden lower lip, moving rhythmically up and down and threatening, as I thought, to start a brush fire at any moment in the facial undergrowth when it burned down to the merest stub. Given the luxuriance of the moustache (mowser, we called it), I never did see how he managed to avoid a conflagration when he lit up one of the ultra-short tabbies that he stored behind one or other of the ears out of which yet more luxuriant hair growth sprouted.

The sparrow incident had clearly taken place somewhere around his backyaird where carrots, kail and tatties grew in rows so straight that you wondered if the vegetables realised that coming up the slightest bit out of line would provoke a good swearing. Only minutes before, I'd seen him with his graip, lifting his crop of 'Majestic' tatties and venting an oath as he inadvertently speared one of his prize harvest. For lining up his rows, he had a length of tow attached between a spike at one end and a more substantial metal object he called the furler at the other. The latter could be whirled round to allow him to draw out the appropriate length when sowing his rows of seeds or planting his dreels of tatties in their regimental lines. At the end of the season it was carefully wound back and put away into in his shed to await the next year's crop preparation. Needless to say, everything in the shed was lined up with the same degree of tidiness and precision. Although I was never actually inside this garden holy of holies, I often peeped in when the door was left open, in awe at the carefully spaced line-up of tools, jars and tins. The wayward ways of crops, like peas, with their wandering tendrils, must have been a sore trial to him but he did his best to keep them in order and encouraged them to climb upwards among twiggy cut branches. When he was out among his vegetables, you almost expected him at any moment to call for order in the ranks.

Still hissing malevolence through his whiskers, he steadfastly ignored the cast iron boot scraper on our doorstep and walked straight into the back lobby, dropping lumps of compacted damp black soil from his soles at regular intervals along the length of the linoleum. My granny wasn't exactly house-proud but the sight of so much garden ground on her lino wasn't to her liking at all. "Mercy, bit ye'll hae half the yaird traillt intil the hoose!" she pronounced with a scowl. The miscreant looked down, eyeing the line of deposits with the imprinted pattern of his sole upon them. "Affa sorry tae be makkin sic a bliddy sotter, mistress" he muttered apologetically, lifting his boot and eyeing the offending sole. My eye was drawn to his wellies. The circular red rubber patches stuck all over the outside to repel the leaks made his worn footwear look as if they'd been afflicted by some form of horticultural contagion. Unearthing the tatties from the loose ground had forced copious amounts of black soil under his horny finger nails, and it was out of his two earthy, cupped hands that a tiny, beady black eye now peeped. I could just see its owner turning a bright yellow head to one side to take note of the unfamiliar surroundings. "An fit de ye think o this, ma loon?" our neighbour asked, with a look of satisfaction and a whistling exhalation of breath that made the end of his fag fairly glow. He stooped to thrust the dirt-ingrained hands under my nose, all the while exhaling puffs of smoke that made my eyes smart. As he slowly opened up his dirt-ingrained hands in an unexpectedly gentle way, he gradually revealed the green, blue and yellow bundle of feathers to which the bright little eye belonged.

I could tell that he was savouring every moment of his tale of rescue, drawing out an account that was already protracted enough with the many colourful inserts of such a seasoned swearer. As the story unfolded, I learned how our macho local gang of dowdy spurgies had apparently taken exception to the colourful fop that had crash-landed in their patch. We heard in graphic detail how the fugitive had been pursued around the garden till at last it sought sanctuary in the privet hedge, probably to a chirruped chorus of derision from the spurgies up on the roof slates. They'd obviously never encountered such an ornithological oddity before and had been determined to make the most of the situation.

When the little yellow face finally pushed its way out between the earthy fingers, it gave me a quizzical look. I was instantly transfixed. After all, it wasn't every day that such an exotic creature appeared down our way. Our domestic wildlife encounters didn't stretch much beyond throwing out a few crumbs for the garden residents, like the blackies and mavises that cheered everybody up with their spring singing. I'd never been to any faraway place to sample the colourful wonders of the natural world; up until then any place beyond a radius of a couple of miles from our house was decidedly far away and entirely unvisited. By today's standards we lived a highly sedentary lifestyle. True, the male neighbours who'd seen active wartime service in far off places could look back upon their own foreign experiences, but many of them chose not to talk about them, preferring to keep what they'd seen and experienced to themselves. In any case, those foreign excursions weren't the sort they'd have gone on out of choice, with machine gun fire and exploding bombs as part of the package. Furthermore, television was still years away and natural history programmes a pleasure yet to come.   But, at that moment, not even the showiest tropical parrot nor the gaudiest bird of paradise could have had me more spellbound. "Weel, fit dae ye think?" he repeated, but I could think of nothing to say. I was awestruck to the point of being speechless.

Now, if my recounting of this event should sound a bit over the top in relation to what might be considered a two-a-penny pet these days, I have to stress that these were the immediate post-war years when the country's budgerigar population was at a low ebb. The nation had been encouraged to keep hens for the sake of turning tattie parings into eggs to supplement the restricted diet, but importing seed for pet birds that couldn't earn their keep hardly ranked as a priority when convoys were being torpedoed out of the Atlantic and the population's very food supply was in jeopardy. Not surprisingly, when seeds became scarce, seed-eating cage birds became thin on the ground along with them. Even some years after the end of hostilities, ownership of such an exotic pet would never have been considered as part of our domestic scene. In the circumstances, the budgie's unexpected arrival was a real bonus and I couldn't have been more excited.

To my delight, my granny expressed no objection to giving a temporary home to the waif. In fact, she seemed genuinely sorry for the "peer birdie" as she was wont to call it forever after. A battered old cage with bent wires and chipped white porcelain pots, one for seed and the other for water, and a wooden swing that dangled lopsidedly from the rusting domed top, was hastily retrieved out of another neighbour's coal shed; It had hung there on a nail since the demise of its last occupant, probably some long-forgotten, pre-war canary. The cage's current squatters were summarily evicted, along with all their festooning webs made black by accumulations of coal stue. After a good clean out, and when two wooden perches had been slotted into place, all was ready for the new tenant. Compared to the modern bird cages you can find in today's pet shops with the latest in deluxe chrome fittings and en-suite extras, this was definitely no parakeet palace but it did offer an adequate home for the refugee.

With no reports of a missing budgie in the vicinity, the fugitive bird became our adoptee and my first pet (unless you count tadpoles and the like). I could have wished to cultivate a closer relationship but quickly learned to keep my fingers well clear of the bars, as he turned out to be of a somewhat cantankerous nature, showing little gratitude for his rescue from the bullying spurgies. In fact, he seldom lost an opportunity to take a sudden nip of any tender young finger flesh that came within range of his sharp beak. I spent hours in studied fascination, sitting alongside the cage out on the front doorstep on the fine days of summer. He looked as if he was enjoying the warmth of the sun on his feathers, dreaming perhaps of his ancestral Aussie homeland. I carefully observed every movement, from his method of shelling the tiny round millet seeds with his hooked beak to the delicate way in which he set about preening the tiniest of feathers. I was entranced by his rich plumage with its bright shades, spots and bars and I could see why the spurgies might have reacted as they did. When he'd burst suddenly into their midst, he must have put them and their drab plumage firmly in the shade. No wonder they'd been miffed when such a colourful stranger entered their world and gave them a real showing up. The yellow face with its flanking black spots was complemented by a bright blue cere above his beak and that, I was told by someone who knew about such matters, was how you could tell that he was indeed a 'he' and not a 'she.' On his back, each dark feather was delicately traced in pale yellow and from his striking green under parts projected a long blue tail. All in all, he was very much the picture of the slim, original aboriginal budgerigar before selective breeding for exhibition at cage bird shows created specimens so top heavy these days that you wonder they don't tumble off their perches. With such colourful plumage, I hardly noticed the general air of scruffiness that had resulted from his duffing-up by the spurgies after his dive into the hedge.

With the passing days it became clear that the fugitive wasn't exactly in the first flush of youth. Perhaps in the evening of his years at his former abode he'd decided to make the flight to freedom that he'd been sitting on his perch dreaming about for long enough; seizing the chance to make one glorious dash through an open window when his cage door was left open. Perhaps the sheer wild excitement of it all had proved too much after years of solitary bachelor existence. At any rate, he had a surprise in store just a few months later. When I crossed the freezing cold lino in my bare feet on a winter morning to pull back the cage's overnight cover, I sensed a deathly silence. Gingerly lifting up the edge of the cloth, I could see the stiff little green corpse lying feet-up on the bottom of the cage. I howled. Our unexpected guest hadn't stayed long with us before moving on to the great budgerigar corroboree in the sky.

Perhaps it was the case that his outback genes weren't hardy enough to cope with the bone-chilling rigour of winter in our draughty old house, but the Sherlock Homes in me later suspected gas poisoning as another possible cause of death.

Whatever the reason: old age, gas poisoning, or a combination of both, the colourful stranger had shuffled off his mortal coil. I inhumed him before sunset in the garden with due dignity, laying him out peacefully on his back with eyes closed and clenched claws pointing heavenwards, in a little cardboard box that I reverently buried among the pansies. While I was digging the grave with the garden trowel, our moustachioed neighbour sidled up and muttered a helpful hint through his whiskers. "If ye dig yer hole doon a twa-three inches mair, ma loon, yer birdie'll be closer til Australia." He slowly stroked the stained grey hairs above his top lip. Remarkably, and perhaps out of respect for the deceased, there was no swearing involved this time. Being of an age to believe implicitly in adult wisdom, I dug the grave just a little bit deeper, as he had suggested, wondering why I caught sight of a wink and noted a hint of inappropriate amusement at such a solemn time.

Looking back on it, I'm sure that the bird that came in from the cold played its part in kindling what was to become a lifelong love for wildlife. I think its unexpected arrival was a bit of a childhood epiphany, an encouragement to open my eyes to what lived around home. Thanks to a brief encounter with a fugitive budgie, I was on the road to becoming a young naturalist.

Chapter 14: Plowterin amang puddocks

As youngsters, our lives were set into the pattern and rhythms of the seasons. We seemed to respond to the lengthening days of spring as much as the creatures that inhabited the country places round about us. We knew, as if by instinct, when it was time to start the annual search for puddocks' eggs, the inert frogspawn that would miraculously transform into fat swimming tadpoles - as long, that is, as the water in the chipped enamel pie dish or the two pound jam jar sitting on the windowsill didn't warm up so much that it cooked its wriggling black occupants on a sunny day.

An agreed Saturday morning was rendezvous time for our all-important expedition to the puddocks' spawning place, Ian, Geordie and myself in standard garb of short breeks, much worn woollen jerseys and black wellies (no fashionable country green then). Equipment for the hunt was of the most basic sort: each of us armed with a jam jar that had a bit of string tied round the rim as a handle for carrying. This yearly appointment in nature's calendar involved a visit to a watery hollow that was almost grown over in spiky green rashes, a good quarter of a mile or so from home along a rutted farm track. No pious visit to a saintly shrine was more faithfully observed than was our springtime pilgrimage to the puddocks' pond. There was always a bit of competition to see who'd be first to spot one of the residents in its watery domain. Somebody would then shout: "I can see ane!" This was the signal that the creatures' camouflage code had been cracked. Then, with your eye attuned, there they were: dozens of unblinking amphibian eyes above greenish-brown backs that barely broke the surface. They were mostly in pairs, the love-struck puddocks, clasping one another in a mating embrace so strong that the smaller males clung resolutely to the backs of their partners even when they plopped under water.

We greeted that first sighting of spawn along the edges with glee, scooping up the slimy extrusions in our hands and letting the thick jelly slither down between our fingers into our jars. "Gyad, it fair pits ye in mind o thon stuff they gie ye for denner at the skweel," was Ian's predictable reaction. He heartily detested tapioca and made a mock show of boaking at the thought of it. For myself, I didn't mind it that much, as long as it came with a good dollop of bright red, home-made rasp jam, the way we had it in our house. Once we'd collected enough of the black-dotted spawn we set out for home, three hunter-gatherers returning in triumph, bearing the day's spoils.

In truth, it wasn't just the spawn collecting that drew us there but the kind of spot it was. Watery places are magnets for children. When you're young there's something about leaving *terra firma* and wading tentatively in among the shallows, with the slightly scary thought that you might disappear into deep water at any moment. "Dinna ye gyang plowterin amang watter!" was my granny's predictable admonition each time I left the house and, just as predictably, I would shake my head in innocent agreement. The countryside had a different look to it in those days. Government drainage grants didn't feature much in the farm scene, so the puddocks could loup, plop and generally laze away their days in their watery haunts, untroubled by anybody wanting to pull the plug on their ancestral wetlands.

But the amphibians' egg laying places weren't theirs alone. The scenes of their amorous spring trysts were remnants of a once greater wild that had now largely gone and so the marshy places had become precious, unofficial little wildlife sanctuaries. They were home to a variety of birds, like the families of moorhens that lived out their nervy, head-jerking lives among the rashes, jinking in and out with bright red and yellow beaks and signalling to one another with flashes of white rump. We didn't see much of these shy water hennies, for they led secretive lives into which human intrusion wasn't welcome. They had the knack of melting mysteriously into the vegetation, providing us with an object lesson in how nature provides her creatures with a mantle of invisibility when required. Occasionally the shy birds were considerate enough to make their nests in places where we could wade without water coming in over the tops of our wellies and saturating our thick, home-knitted socks. Locating a nest was an opportunity to admire the clutch of matching brown-blotched eggs and we were pleased with ourselves when we chanced upon the elusive prize.

When Providence smiled on our long summer holidays and the days were especially warm and sunny, the three of us weren't the only ones to defy all warnings and sneak off down to the slow winding river. Some older loons were daring enough to strip off their clothes and dook, stark naked, in the deeper pools where the big fish rose and spread big ripples over the surface. The sunshine sparkled on the water but, once your eyes became accustomed, you could pick out big speckled trout with their noses pointed upstream into the flow like underwater weather vanes. Moving their tails lazily back and fore, they somehow kept their bodies steady against the force of the current. Where the sunshine warmed the shallows, little shoals of bandies, the name we used for their tiny progeny, darted about among our bare toes, stirring up clouds of muddy water as they sped off in panic into the green water weed. Grumpy craggie herons lifted lankily from the edge of the river bank, flapping grudgingly away and croaking their irritation at the unwelcome disturbance to their solitary fishing, while dapper black and white watery wagtails bobbed their tails uncontrollably up and down in an endless chasing after insects along the muddy margins. One of our best moments came the summer day when a black cow ambled across from its field on the opposite bank to slake its thirst. When the beast ventured on to a section that had been undermined by the winter spates, what was obvious to us on from our side wasn't so obvious to the cow. With the whole weight of the well-fed animal on the overhang the sandy bank collapsed, sending the startled creature thrashing about in wild panic in the water till at last it managed to scramble back up again and race across its field to reflect on the indignity of what had happened.

No country lane within a radius of a mile or two of home was unvisited territory in our wanderings and we must have been a familiar sight to the folk who passed along them. With no TV and no computers around to absorb our time we were free as birds to wander about and enjoy ourselves in the open air. After the short hours of daylight in winter, the lengthening days of spring allowed us to roam further afield. In the countryside calendar, March was the month when the teuchats came back from wherever it was they'd passed their winter days, crying and tumbling in their excited display flights like slow-flapping, big black and white butterflies. Shortly afterwards, they were united in their pair bonds and making their nest scrapes on the bare brown parks whose edges were starting to yellow with the bursting buds of the whins. They had a variety of names, those familiar occupants of the farmlands. At home, we called them teuchats but to others they were peesies or peesie-weeps from the calls they made, and in the bird book on our classroom nature table they went by the name of lapwing and the even grander name of green plover. In an age when farming and bird life coexisted in a more intimate way, a farmer out harrowing a ploughed field would signal to his pair of horse to stop if an incubating bird rose up and cried out in alarm. Once he'd lifted up the clutch of four pointed, brown-spotted eggs and put them into his bonnet, the eggs could be carefully placed back together on to the ground, safe from the horses' hooves. In this simple act, the harmony of man and wild creature was reaffirmed and the bird's future in the farmlands was secure.

But nature could be fickle in her dealings with the teuchats. Sometimes the earliest nesters were caught out by a sudden, unexpected return of wintry weather. As swirls of snowflakes danced wildly about in the unwelcome Arctic blasts, the old mannies would shake their heads and observe gravely "Aye, that'll be the teuchats' storm," for these unwelcome last gasps of winter had come to be named after the birds. As April days passed and the calendar slipped into another month, things were meant to get better but sometimes there came one last chilly spell which our elders knew as the Gab o Mey. But no matter how bad the weather we were experiencing at home, the swallows had already set out on their long, northwards journey back from Africa, returning to age-old nesting sites among cobweb-covered rafters in byres and sheds. Once the first cheery twitter was heard in the skies overhead, people took the time to look up and comment "The swallas are back! Simmer's surely comin." That first sighting was worthy of note; a welcome bit of news, as if the birds' reappearance was a guarantee of the fine days' return. If the passage of the year was like the pages in a book, then folk regarded that first, excited swallow twitter as a key marker in them.

As the last expressions of spring gave way to the leafy days of summer, we could hardly wait for the holidays to come, all thought of school put away for seven long, carefree weeks of summer excursions. With a bottle of fizzy ale from the lemonade lorry that came round the doors with its rattling wooden crates and a couple of slices of buttered loaf in a piece tin, we were happy to forego mid-day mealtimes and just plowtered to our hearts' content in the burns and dawdled along farm tracks flanked by lichen-encrusted dykes. The big stones, laboriously lifted and carted off the parks in years long gone, had been made into dykes to consume what had been dumped thousands of years before by the retreating ice sheet. Half-smoothed boulders peppered the parks in an abundance that must have sorely tried the patience of countless farming generations. Season after season of their forebears' toil and sweat had moved the equivalent of mountains off the face of the land, clearing the way for productive agriculture, though each succeeding generation of farmers found that winters of hard frosts brought more big stones up to the surface to take the place of the ones they'd already carted away.

Where the dykes were broad enough, the tops sometimes became our own highway through the farmlands, as we paused to disentangle a jersey sleeve from a wild raspberry cane, or to tie a pint that had lowsened in a well-scuffed tackety beet. We wandered unhindered along lanes and tracks that were little troubled by traffic, and what there was generally tended to move at a fairly slow pace anyway. We were growing up in an age of innocence, when road safety issues were of no great concern and when nobody at home was troubled that we might be lured away by some paedophile lurking behind a dyke or hawthorn hedge (not that anyone round our way would have had the slightest notion what the word meant).

I'd no access to books at home to help identify the birds that made their homes nearby. The Pilgrim's Progress, the Bible, a thick blue-bound volume of Burns' poetry, a small dictionary and a well thumbed copy of Pears Cyclopaedia, with its worn red spine hanging off, made up our entire collection. This modest home library was housed on one side of the fire in an unpainted wooden box that my granny had obtained for a few pennies from the grocer and which still smelled of the fruits that had once made the journey across from the orange groves of the sunny

Mediterranean. Stood up on its end, the middle division and the bottom acted as a handy bookcase. In a sense I suppose I'd almost no need for a bird reference book since the names and knowledge of local species were passed on as a matter of course from generation to generation. I'd long since learned to identify the bright yellow cock yalla yities that perched on top of flowering yellow whin bushes, endlessly singing "A little bit of bread and no chee-eese!" At least, that's what the teacher told us in class that the yellow hammers sang, and that's what it said in her bird book, but the fact was that the word 'bread' wasn't in everyday vocabulary round our way. Breid was what we called oatcakes and white bread was loaf, causing me to wonder why the birds in our part of the world should be singing in such 'proper' language and not in the local way of saying things in the countryside where they resided. It seemed to me that the jaunty little birds should really be singing "A little bittie loaf an nae chee-eese!"

I knew rose linties from their bright pink breasts. The dapper little cock birds perched on broom bushes and sang cheery, twittering songs from the top strands of barbed wire fences, while along the edges of the small woods I became adept at spotting the twiggy nests of cushie doos. They seemed quite feckless home builders at times, these fat pigeons of the woods, hardly bothering themselves about construction techniques when they put together their twiggy platform nests. If the farmlands were the domain of the teuchats, the un-reclaimed remnants of bog ground were where the whaups with their long, downward curving beaks laid their brown marked eggs among the rashes. I'm sure their bubbling, plaintive calling must have entered into my soul at that time as I've never tired of hearing that most haunting and evocative of sounds. Even now, I invariably stop and listen whenever I hear a distant curlew as it breaks the lonely silence of a summer tramp among the hills.

Like a sponge, I absorbed fact after fact about the natural world and the creatures that inhabited it in a thirst that's never been assuaged to this day. I learned not to get too close to a swan on its nest, something I tried once. I ran off in fright when the bird raised its long neck and bright orange bill and gave a menacing hiss. 'Everybody knew' that an encounter with an irate swan was bound to result in a broken arm if it assailed you with its all-powerful wing, so it was best not to take any chances. I found out the hard way that an attack by clegs on a summer evening could leave you with an uncomfortable reminder of the encounter for days to come. Get a few bites on the backs of your bare legs and you knew all about it in the heat under the blankets at night as you tried alternately scratching and not scratching to try to get relief from the irritating itch. I knew all about nature being red in tooth and claw after seeing a sparrow hawk strike like a missile at a doo on the edge of a belt of fir trees, reducing the streamlined bird to an untidy swirl of soft grey feathers. Though I didn't think about it at the time, there were two teachers at work in guiding my burgeoning interest: the one with the zeal for imparting fact within the confines of her old fashioned classroom and the other, nature herself, with her store of wonders in the fresh air and freedom of the country places.

Chapter 15: Forkietails and futrats

My granny seemed to have some lingering, primeval fear of the power of the elements. That's the only way I can explain her reaction to thunder and lightning. The merest, distant clap of thunder, no matter how faint, was enough to trigger the same response. If she was engaged in conversation, she would break off in mid sentence and cup her hand behind her ear. "Harken!" she'd say, with undisguised apprehension, "ah doot there'll be thunner an lichtnin here yet." There was real foreboding in her voice as she set about preparing to defend the house against impending doom. If she happened to be in the middle of baking, she'd lay down her rolling pin and lift the sash window with floury hands, jamming it open with the small piece of wood that rested on the sill for that purpose. There was a degree of urgency about things. This was a matter far too important to wait; the very future of our household was at risk.

Once the matter of the window was attended to, the ritual of the mirror could be enacted. This involved turning it round to make the reflecting side face the wall. The logic seemed to be that any lightning intent on mischief might be attracted inside by the shiny surface, so the obvious thing was to avoid taking chances before the thunder moved too close. She had a mortal dread of a bolt from the blue travelling down our lum and creating mayhem inside the house. By her reckoning, if the unwelcome visitor did succeed in gaining entry, it would find its way out again as long as the window was left open. Well, that was the theory of it anyway and there was no point in even beginning to question the scientific credibility of any of it, especially if you were my age. It was just what she did and always had done, and what her ancestors had no doubt done before, so that was that. But even my brain, in its state of prepubescent immaturity, was left wondering why something as immensely powerful as lightning would need a window to be left open for it. The response would almost certainly have been "Weel, weel, bit that's jist the wye o't, ma loon," as indeed it was to anything that wasn't easily explained but just **was**.

As youngsters, we acquired our own beliefs. It was part of the process of growing up in our time and place. One belief we had involved the tall *umbellifers* that bloomed along every roadside in early summer days with so many frothy white flower heads that the verges looked as if they'd been covered in an unseasonable fall of snow. We called them thunner flooers and believed that knocking them over would bring down the rain as surely as if you'd stamped on a worm. That being the way of things, they were best left to bloom in peace in the interests of avoiding unwanted precipitation. After all, what was the point of risking a change from a fine, dry summer's day to a spell of pouring rain when you'd just be forced to stay inside the house? Here was a case of 'best not to tamper with nature' if ever there was one. If you'd thoughtlessly decapitated one of the flower heads with a stick earlier in the day you might be left wondering, in a guilty sort of way, whether you might just have been responsible for the heavy plump of rain that later soaked the clothes on the washing line at home.

Other beliefs were seamlessly stitched into the fabric of our childhood and I never gave them a second thought till much later on in life. Some, I realise now, were probably more adult inventions of expediency than anything else, like the story that was put into our highly impressionable minds that one nearby pond was so deep that it had no bottom. Tumble into that, we were told, and you'd be sinking down into its dark depths forever. It was a prospect scary enough to keep us from venturing too near, which was presumably the whole point of that particular tarradiddle.

Beliefs about the natural world were passed on from generation to generation, like the idea that forkietails, alias hornie-gollachs, alias earwigs, were adept at finding their way into your ears, with potentially dire consequences. Should you happen to fall asleep out of doors on a summer's day with your ear to the ground, the risk level would naturally be heightened. If a forkie gained entry, there was no telling the havoc it might wreak within the confines of the aural orifice but the most likely thing was that your brain would be the first target of the pincer-like things at the end of its body, so it was best to take no chances. It was probably because of this particular belief that I was never all that keen on handling a forkie, though they were interesting creatures to look at as they came in all shades of shiny brown, with even an occasional pure white specimen. They lived in fences and under flat bits of wood on the ground. As soon as you lifted a piece and let the daylight in, the forkies, along with the slaters and shiny black beetles that cohabited in the dark places, scuttled about in confusion not knowing what to do when the brightness suddenly broke in upon their secret world. I used to feel sorry for causing them such confusion and made sure that their roof went back in place after I'd had a look.

The thought of a forkie crawling inside your lug was bad enough, but the merest glimpse of a futrat was enough to send a shiver down the spine, especially if you were out in the countryside on your own and the beast popped up at close quarters. These stoats were lithe, furtive creatures that darted in and out among the lichen-covered boulders of the drysteen dykes, stopping for a moment to lift their heads and sniff the air before disappearing again. This was one creature that the three of us definitely weren't comfortable with as we'd all heard the stories about what might happen if you found yourself surrounded by a whole pack of them, an act of nature which, admittedly, none of us had actually yet came across (let alone heard of anyone who'd ever been molested by a whole menacing gang of them). If the worst did happen, you might as well resign yourself to a fate too horrible to contemplate since 'everybody knew' that they would spring up at you and sink their teeth into your windpipe and that would be that. It was a shame that we viewed them with such suspicion and dread as they were such beautiful creatures in their sleek brown and white coats. Maybe it was yet another tale put about to frighten us away from unstable dykes that might tumble down and cause injury if we played on top of them. In the cold days, if you were lucky, you might get a glimpse of one of the animals in its white winter coat with a black tip to its tail. We learned in class from our teacher (never one to miss an opportunity to communicate her interest in all things royal) that the monarchs of the realm wore cloaks decorated with futrat tails, only she didn't call them that. As kingly garb they had a much grander name. Somehow 'futrat fur' just didn't have the same cachet as 'ermine' for a ceremonial garment at a coronation or some such regal affair.

*****

In the age I'm speaking about here, folk were more in tune with weather matters and constantly looking for signs of what the elements might have in store. After all, weather impacted directly on lives and livelihoods in rural parts. Red rowan berries were taken as indicators of the winter weather to come. Whilst you could hear folk admiring the heavy red clusters that weighed the branches down, the display of nature's bounty was also the cause of much head shaking and uttering of dire predictions of how bad things might turn out to be in the winter days ahead. This doom and gloom mentality was a speciality of the male village elders who had all the time in the world to take note of such things and then use them to spread their own brand of despondency around the place. It was seen at its best, or worst, in the dour warning "Ah doot we'll pey for't yet" when we had a really fine spell, as though the Almighty would be expecting some payback for His gift of fine days.

The group of pipe-smoking old men who occupied the wooden bench seats in the centre of town and kept a check on everybody's comings and goings were especially given to this sort of thing, punctuating their dire predictions with well-aimed spits of tobacco juice. Just as nature abhors a vacuum, so they seemed to abhor any silence when they sat together. When they weren't actually newsin or engaged in spreading doom and gloom, they went into a distinctive idling mode where long, silent pauses in conversation were punctuated by the occasional "Aye" or "Imph", or "Weel, weel"; interruptions that had no great meaning on their own but perhaps served to communicate to one another that they were actually still living and breathing. Their theory about the rowan berries was that nature was one step ahead and was intent on providing a bumper food supply to see the birds through the harsh winter days to come. No one seemed to recognise the more plausible connection that optimum weather conditions earlier in the year might have been responsible for the berry bonanza.

Some of my granny's ideas were certainly deeply ingrained. Her belief in the value of a good weekly purge as an aid to healthy living is all too vividly burned into my mind. The ritual involved the regular administration of a dose of the singularly vile substance called liquid paraffin which performed much the same function as syrup of figs. This was a taste to top all tastes on the scale of nastiness. The colourless, oily substance was dispensed by the droggist into a clear bottle. A large white label was then licked and stuck on to the side, bearing the somewhat unhelpful instruction **To be taken as required.** My granny had as great a dread of constipation as she had of thunder and lightning and took **'as required'** to mean a generous weekly dose.

She also swore by the value of a hot fomentation if I was unfortunate enough to be beset by a boil or some related affliction. This drastic action would probably constitute torture under European law these days and be outlawed as a form of child abuse, though the procedure was carried out with the best of intentions. It was performed in time honoured fashion with the aid of a poultice, made by soaking a piece of bread of appropriate dimension in near boiling milk, then applying it at top speed to the affected spot on whatever part of the anatomy it might be located. The effect of such concentrated heat, whether on neck or backside, made you jump as much as if you'd been connected up to mains electricity (which, of course, we weren't). The theory was that the searing heat would draw out the badness and get rid of any matter welling up under the skin. If I was unfortunate enough to be afflicted by anything deemed worthy of a bread poultice, I just had to hope that the one treatment would prove effective and avoid the necessity for another scalding hot application. A related sort of complaint known as a blin lump was in a class of its own and reluctant to yield to any application of steaming-hot soaked bread.

* * * * *

Summer days seemed deliciously long. During the long school holidays, our three small forms might be seen outdoors till the sun dipped down and the damp air of nightfall filled the howe with trailing wisps of mist. Sometimes we joined up with the quines for hide and seek or any other game that needed greater numbers to be worth playing. At other times we searched among the grass for a lucky four-leaved clover, dreaming of the untold wealth in sweetie money that might come our way if we actually found one. We blew away the fluffy seeds from dandelion clocks and used them to tease one another regarding a supposed amorous link with some quine in class that you probably couldn't stick the sight of. We also carried out the age old test for a liking for butter by putting an open buttercup flower under one another's chins, though the fact was that when the yellow of the flower appeared in reflection, it was more likely to be an indication of a greasy, unwashed neck rather than anything else.

When it came to beliefs regarding human reproduction, speculation inevitably attended the arrival of a bairn into a family, especially if it was a new brother or sister for someone we knew. When a woman was said to be expectin, the word was invariably uttered in hushed tones if young ears were around, which only heightened the intrigue and made the topic the more interesting to enquiring young minds. When the teacher asked a boy in our class one day to explain an absence, his face reddened more and more till at last he blurted out "Ma mither's expectin." Mind you, the embarrassed woman's face turned an awful lot redder than the boy's and, just to make matters worse, she couldn't even chastise him in the usual way for his use of Doric. To do so would have meant her changing the word to 'expecting,' which wouldn't have sounded right anyway, and uttering it in class would certainly have offended her sense of decorum.

Any new birth was a subject worthy of discussion in our little circle. It goes without saying that the three of us had heard mention of storks being responsible for new arrivals but we were sceptical in the extreme. "Weel, **a've** nivver seen ane fleein aboot the place;" averred Ian, "nae even fan ma wee brither cam intil the hoose." Geordie and I were of the shared opinion that if the birds **had** been about they must have flown in under cover of darkness since none of us could say that we'd actually sighted one in the vicinity of any house nearby, where the sudden appearance of a white line of hippens on a washin tow was the certain indication of a new birth. The nearest things to storks we ever saw were the long-necked craggie herons that stalked along the burns and fished down by the river and it was only a trootie that might be spotted in their long beaks; never a sign of even the tiniest infant.

The fact was that we suspected there might be more to such matters than met the eye. Unseen stork deliveries and babies left under gooseberry bushes seemed improbable explanations, no matter that this was all that adults were prepared to come up with. Besides, in our countryside ramblings we'd observed with glee the mountings of cows by amorous bulls, and had an inkling that calves somehow appeared later as a result, creating a suspicion that the arrival of human babies had an explanation that was other than something to do with gooseberry bushes and storks that passed in the night. Geordie was heartily sick of hearing a story told against him. When he was very little, his mother produced an addition to the family in the shape of a wee brother. The newborn had just arrived in the room upstairs and his father came down to announce the good news. Geordie's excitement at the prospect of having an instant playmate in the house was dampened when his father cautioned, "Oh, bit he winna be able tae rin aboot," whereupon a concerned wee Geordie had innocently asked, "Fit wye, Da? His the bairnie nae got ony legs?" This seemed to occasion much mirth among the adults, but after a while of hearing the story told over and over again, Geordie had ceased to see any funny side to it and just glowered every time his father told the tale afresh.

Chapter 16: Living with nature

When summer clouds parted and the days were fine, I loved when the butterflies took to the wing and basked in the sunshine. As yet, their numbers hadn't been depleted by the intensification of agriculture, especially the spraying of pesticides and herbicides. The countryside used to be a friendlier place for insects because it was a haven for the plants on which their lives depended. Early summer days were a delight, when the rich yellow on the broom gave way to a colourful show of wild flowers. Even humble neep parks were magically transformed into eye-catching squares of yellow by the unrestrained blooming of skelloch. It must have been an insect heaven.

There must have been another vestige of the hunting instinct within us when we chased after the fast flying insects with nothing more than a jam jar and lid or a bandy net. Butterflies were perverse creatures, sitting still for hardly a minute, cunningly waiting till you got just within striking range then taking to the air and fluttering off into the distance. Needless to say, the flightier they were the more determined we became. It was one of the trials of nature that the creatures had a special liking for the patches of creeping thistles that spread over patches of waste ground. And, in a double dose of perversity, they liked to lay their eggs on the jobbie nettles that flourished around farm muck middens. If, in the heat of the chase, you happened to brush a bare leg against a patch of nettles, it was no use dashing home for some soothing cream. Instead, in the manner of the ancients, we cast our eyes around for a broad docken leaf to give the rash a good rub to assuage the stinging.

There was nothing scientific about our butterfly classification. 'Fyte eens' were generally the large white ones which plagued gardeners with their habit of gluing tiny yellow eggs to the undersides of the leaves of cabbages, kale or cauliflowers. However, it's an ill wind, as they say, and when things reached plague proportions in fine weather, it was occasionally possible to earn an income of a few pennies from neighbouring gardeners for searching for the hairy black and green caterpillars that chewed their destructive way along the leaves. I recall no suggestion of additional 'dirty' money for getting fingers stained with the foul smelling green liquid expelled by the creatures as their ultimate deterrent, but I do remember having to counter the strong smell of cabbage-rich caterpillar excretion afterwards with a good hand washing in the sink at home using a bar of pungent carbolic soap.

The ones we called 'broon eens' were mostly the small tortoiseshell variety with colours and wing markings more varied and attractive than our name would suggest. They required more careful stalking when they sat at rest with their wings wide open on the purple thistle flowers, soaking up the summer warmth. You had to watch your step when you tried to get up close to these flighty sun worshippers. Just when you were ready to pounce, a carelessly placed shadow was enough to make them flit off to some even pricklier patch and you had to begin the stalking process all over again. And so we learned the advantage of stealth, being careful to watch where we stood in relation to the sun. In late summer days, a bright red admiral was a special prize. The tiny, bright blue butterflies were less common and tended to be a lot smarter than suffer the indignity of letting themselves be put into a jar, albeit for a short while. We didn't go in much for capturing bumble bees, otherwise known as bummers. Any time we did, they expressed their extreme annoyance by generating enough buzzing to set the sides of the jar reverberating. It was quite scary feeling their anger being transmitted through the glass into your fingers. The big, hairy black and yellow foggie bummers were none too pleased about being stared at. Neither were their cousins with the prominent reddish backsides, the ones we called descriptively, if slightly rudely, reed ersies.

For the purposes of our butterfly hunts, jars had to be spirited away out of the press at home, since they were used over and over again in the domestic jam making process. For my study purposes they were ideal see-through containers. In our household, a jar in which I'd had an interesting looking snail one month might have a fill of rhubarb jam in it the next and nobody was any the wiser after I'd quietly replaced it among the other jars. There was also an abundance of the more earthbound members of creation. Despite the lack of cooperation on the part of the creatures, we never gave up on our attempts at organising slater races on a flat bit of ground. These were generally doomed to failure since the creatures had no sense of a straight line. In fact, they weren't obliging in the least, making off in every direction but the one they were meant to follow. The more sensible among them remained curled up in a tight ball, steadfastly refusing to budge and not entering into the spirit of things at all. Trying to persuade a brown maggie mony-feet (scientifically answering to the name of centipede) to enter a jar was an even greater challenge, as the creature's over generous endowment of legs allowed it to shift at the speed of light. The more you tried to catch it, the more it turned into a futile exercise. Should one of the fast shifting creatures deign to enter, the trick was to get the lid on quick before it did one of its Houdini acts and shot back out and away under the nearest stone. I suppose you could hardly blame such free living residents of the wild for not wanting to cooperate when you tried to put them where they didn't want to be. Washer wifies were a particular frustration. This was our name for the long-legged pond skaters that seemed to have perfected the trick of sitting just above the water surface in what appeared to be a demonstration of insect levitation. It wasn't hard to find washer wifies since they inhabited every still bit of water surface, but it was a real frustration to try and catch one, as they had a habit of shooting off like multi-legged Olympic speed skaters.

*****

In these post-war years, housing availability and quality were a matter of concern. Things were starting to improve slowly but there were some decidedly sub-standard dwellings that were still being lived in, not excluding our own. However, this was nothing compared with an old cottage that the three of us occasionally passed on our country forays. The tumbledown place stood on its own, a distance away from any near neighbours. It was inhabited by a cheery old craitur who didn't seem to miss company. Summer or winter, she seemed to appear in the same worn old wellies. She didn't have the luxury of a mains water supply, so fetching the water in a pail from her well was probably what kept her fit; that and the digging of her garden and the tattie planting. In summer there was a dark red rose in front of the house with a perfume you could smell from yards away when the air was warm and still. There was no running water; the well was round the back. Folk said that down in its dark depths dwelt a troot whose task was to keep the water clean by disposing of all the creepie crawlies unlucky enough to tumble down from above. The deep-dwelling fish obviously had to work for its supper but I did wonder about the next stage after it had obligingly consumed the offending animal life. The most cursory glance into my goldfish's bowl on the windowsill above the sink was enough to realise that what went in one end of a fish must of necessity come out the other, and in less appealing form. No matter how thirsty, I would never have fancied the idea of a drink from that particular source with its accumulated evacuation of piscine bowels.

It wasn't only in the matter of housing that change was in the air. When you're young you tend to accept things and think nothing much about them, but these were times when the countryside was undergoing technological advance. Farming had been progressing from animal to mechanical motive power for some time but the process was still far from complete, especially on the smaller farms. There was no finer sight than on a brisk March day when a white flurry of black-headed gulls descended behind a ploughman and his Clydesdale pair, the noisy birds hardly taking time to swallow the newly exposed worms. Inside the old stone-built dwellings, bathrooms were a luxury unknown, while bare flagstone floors were still a feature of some farm houses. In one that I sometimes called in past, the boldest of the farmyard hens used to come in the open door and search for crumbs under the kitchen table. Such places were fated to change as farming became more intensive and the economics of running small enterprises didn't stack up, even though a large measure of self sufficiency was still the order of the day. Self sufficiency was also a built-in part of our daily living at home and food waste was an abomination to my granny. In the absence of a fridge, things naturally went off more readily in summer but she would simply brush off the odd bit of blue hairy mould and nobody seemed to die as a result. "Ye've tae ate a ton o dirt afore ye dee," was one of her much used aphorisms.

On our forays into the countryside we enjoyed an easy relationship with the farmers. They probably regarded us with a benign indifference, recognising that we did no harm. But there was one who took exception to our presence in one of his parks at harvest time. As a rule, we respected boundaries and didn't intrude too much into farmland but on this fine autumn day we succumbed to temptation. "We could gyang in an play amang the stooks," suggested Geordie and off the three of us duly trooped, squeezing through the strands of fence wire. No doubt we'd recently been to one of the Saturday afternoon matinees at the cinema and been treated to a good going gun fight in a cowboy film. Hiding behind the upstanding oat stooks, we were soon absorbed in a scenario that involved pretend guns and plenty of simulated gunfire, generating the kind of noises that kids are good at making on such occasions. I daresay one or two sheaves may have become a bit displaced as the firing became more intense and we dodged from stook to stook, avoiding the bullets. Anyway, the racket must have been loud enough to attract the attention of the farmer, and so engrossed were all of us gunslingers that we didn't hear him approach till he let fly with a verbal salvo of his own. "Cam ower here if ye want yer little erses kickit!" he shouted. Seeing the black looks on his florid face, it was an offer the three of us could easily refuse and we took to our heels. As we struggled to escape between the taught strands of wire, he clearly wanted to demonstrate that it had been no idle threat. Free of the wire, I turned round just in time to see him aim his boot in the direction of Geordie's fleeing posterior which was momentarily wedged between the wires. At this, the farmer's wellie flew off and he was left hopping about in red-faced, apoplectic rage. When we passed that particular place in future we always kept a wary eye in case he should be harbouring a grudge and come after us again, this time with more firmly secured footwear.

*****

Our names for wildlife could be much more expressive than the ones found in any bird identification book. Oystercatchers, for example, were skirlie wheeters, earning their name from their shrill calling. I could hear them at night when I lay in bed as they made their way up the valley in late winter. This was the season when thoughts of pairing up were coming into their heads. The first time I saw one of the smart black and white birds close up was among the gravestones in a neatly maintained cemetery. It was struggling to pull a big worm out of the short turf with its long red beak. The worm's elasticity was presenting it with a real challenge but eventually the long wriggling shape yielded and it (or a part of it at least), came up out of the soft ground. I was mightily impressed and never forgot the sight of it.

Compared to such a dapper bird, the ever present spurgies were as plain as they come. But in spite of their dowdiness, they were probably my favourites. In the springtime, the little male birds danced around the rooftops after the females, their tails cocked up and their wings dropped in their own amorous display, repeating the same chirruping sound over and over again. As courtship progressed, the sight of one bird quivering on the back of another became commonplace, providing us with a bit of a clue to the mechanics of reproduction. Sometimes a cock bird would appear in triumph with a downy white hen's feather in his beak, making him look like he had a little white beard.

Birds were a familiar part of our everyday scene and more folk could put a name to the different ones than tends to be the way today. Even so, our knowledge of them was anything but an exact science. When noisy black gatherings of hundreds of birds passed high over the house before sundown on a summer's evening, I was informed by my granny that "They're awa tae a craas' weddin." When I looked up, I could see the birds wheeling and tumbling so jovially about the sky that they certainly did look as though they were setting out to enjoy themselves, but it was much later that I realised that what my granny took to be corvid nuptials were really gatherings before the rooks (for such they were) took themselves off to the high branches of some nearby

129

craas' widdie to roost for the night. Their magpie cousins that built their domed nests out of reach inside prickly hawthorn bushes were regarded as cunning birds with a dubious reputation, while their smaller, sharp-eyed relations, the jackdaws, were under suspicion as opportunist thieves.

Poaching in the countryside was regarded as a legitimate activity by some of our male neighbours. They viewed it simply as a way of providing for the pot and were wily enough not to be caught by the gamekeepers when they were out with their shotguns. From time to time, and generally after a moonlit winter's night, a wild dyeuk that had spent the previous day dabbling happily among the marshland down by the river ended up as a lifeless corpse in the morning on my granny's table awaiting plucking. It was on such an occasion that I was first entranced by the wonder of iridescence as I stroked the smooth feathering on the limp head of a mallard drake. As I did so, the shining green head caught the morning sunshine that was streaming in above the low white screens on the window. It was an intensity of colour that I'd never appreciated before in any bird. The magical way in which the colour changed from green to black and back again according to the way it caught the light seemed to me to be truly one of nature's miracles.

Chapter 17: School slates and stinky sponges

I've realised that I'm old enough to say that my schooling began, if not quite in the Stone Age then certainly in the age of stone. When my classmates and I took our first tentative steps on the road to writing we had neither jotters nor lead pencils for our school work. Instead, in the manner of the ancients who scratched their petroglyphs on to the walls of their caves, our earliest efforts in class were committed to stone, in our case a thin piece of slate set into a square wooden frame. At a time of post-war austerity there was no question of the school wasting paper on the uncertain scrawls of learner novice writers like myself. When you think about it, the classroom stack of slates was a model of sustainable use of resources in education since the natural material could be used over and over again. Several decades on, with the price of school stationery ever increasing, education authorities might well be wondering if they should be trying to negotiate a deal with a slate quarrier somewhere. There was the down side, of course, in that they were much noisier to use than jotters, not least when somebody made a careless stack of them and the whole lot came clattering down on to the floor, to our teacher's extreme annoyance.

On the teacher's desk sat an old cardboard chalk box with some worn stumps of slate pencil but you were really meant to bring your own. This was also a piece of slate, this time shaped like a thin pencil, with a bit of coloured paper wrapping round its middle. You could buy one for a few pennies at the local stationer's, a shop that smelt deliciously of reams and quires of new paper and had shelves that were overflowing in writing pads and envelopes, ledgers and account books, squat bottles of Stephen's ink, large scrapbooks and sheets of brightly coloured scraps for sticking into them. The glossy scraps were sold in sheets and could be easily detached from one another for sticking on to a page. They covered all manner of themes from fierce wild animals from faraway jungles to colourful birds, flowers, farm machines and the latest flashy American automobiles, the fancy word our trans-Atlantic cousins used for their cars. Scraps were popular at the time; less popular was the taste left on your tongue from the fishy glue on their reverse side and you wished you hadn't been quite so thorough in your licking.

Some school sounds and smells are never forgotten, lodged forever in the recesses of the mind, recalled only when something causes them unexpectedly to surface. Some of mine have to do with slates. To write on one you needed a firm hand to make a whitish score on the smooth grey-blue surface. One side had a permanently marked grid of small squares for doing sums and the other was covered in feint parallel lines which were supposed to keep your writing from wandering off in directions it wasn't meant to take. When a slate pencil was drawn across the face of the slate it did two things. One, it made the intended mark and two, it sometimes created a ghastly screeching noise that was guaranteed to set the teacher's teeth on edge. It hardly needs saying that we quickly mastered the art of making more of the nerve-jarring sound than was absolutely necessary. The poor woman must have been driven demented when a whole lot of slate pencils were scraping and screeching away at the same time.

In this technological age, anyone who wasn't brought up to use a slate for school work might be wondering what happened when you wanted to change a wrong spelling or a sum that didn't add up properly. The answer was simplicity itself. With a wet cloth and a bit of rubbing, hey presto and the white mark disappeared. I felt I'd gone up-market when my granny bought me a small yellow sponge for slate cleaning purposes. This was none of the modern synthetic things but a soft yellow natural sponge from the droggist's. During the shop visit, I'd been distracted by the sight of some intriguingly long yellow loofahs, items whose use was a complete mystery to me. When I turned round, it was to find my granny with a small sponge in her hand. These things would normally be too expensive to be used for such a menial purpose as cleaning a school slate and I wondered if she'd experienced a sudden rush of blood to the head. But the fact was that she'd spotted a bargain. The sponge was priced at only a penny or so because it came out of the bargain basket sitting on the varnished wooden floor. Compared to the full-price specimens piled up in a box on the counter, it was less than perfect. It had come apart at the edges, hence its knock-down price, but it served its unconventional purpose and was a cut above the bits of old sark tail, or whatever my classmates used. I was really pleased with my sponge which had begun its life in the blue waters of the Mediterranean or some other such exotic place. When I took a sniff at it, I even fancied that I could smell something of the warm seas about it.

You'd only take a sniff at a slate cleaning sponge when it was new, however. Things underwent a dramatic change after a week or two in the damp confines of my battered old metal soap dish. To avoid a build-up of the appalling sour smell that resulted from days of airless incarceration, we were supposed to wash our slate cleaning materials at home to avoid sending our poor teacher towards further distraction, but the loons seldom did. Being subjected to the disagreeable odour rising from a whole lot of sour smelling materials must have further tested all powers of endurance. Boys being boys, the idea of using a moist cloth (or sponge) in any case seemed an awful lot of effort when a good spit would do just as well. Besides, being contrary to class rules, it was that bit more daring. So we became adept at spitting on our errors, then erasing them with the aid of our jersey cuffs.

The technique was to hold on to the end of your sleeve, do a quick spit on your mistake and then rub quietly away. Naturally, such an unhygienic practice was anathema to our teacher. Slate spitting was a heinous class crime; a definite no-go and so you had to be furtive about it. If you thought she wasn't looking, you might get away with it but, after years in the classroom, she'd grown eyes on the back of her head and the consequences of being spotted doing a spit were entirely predictable. A rap over the back of your hand from a ruler was enough to make you think twice about the spit and rub approach to slate cleansing for a while.

Some well meaning former pupil sent over a fancy ruler one Christmas as a present for the class. It was formed from a selection of the different kinds of trees that grow in New Zealand. The ruler was a work of art with its different coloured squares of *kauri* and the rest but it didn't meet with our approval at all. It was just our luck that New Zealand happened to be a land of such solid timbers. Years later, when I stood at the solid base of a tall *kauri* tree in New Zealand's North Island, I found it difficult to concentrate on its magnificence. Instead, I was thinking of how one of its compatriots had given its all to be part of an implement of classroom chastisement.

*****

I feel a sense of gratitude that some of the seeds of my love of wildlife were sown for me in my early days in school. Our teacher evidently had her own interest in nature, taking delight in reading us stories of intrepid explorers in scary sounding jungles and their inevitable encounters with ferocious beasts. She had a permanent nature table set out at one side of the room with all manner of bits and pieces, from shiny cowry shells and faded dead corals to old birds' nests. According to the season, she brightened the table with a jar of wild flowers and sometimes she endeavoured to pass on their names by providing little labels. In spring, a small glass tank was brought out of the cupboard to house tadpoles and there was never any shortage of offers to find some frogspawn. In time, we watched the little black specks wriggle out of their blobs of jelly and followed their progress towards metamorphosis. When legs began to appear, it was time to take pity on them and tip them back out into the wild to continue their progress towards full froghood.

To me, the nature table was a constant source of interest and I was always keen to bring in bits and pieces to add to the display, though you had to be careful not to overdo things for fear of earning the unenviable 'teacher's pet' label. I couldn't draw to save my life and admired the ones whose talent lay in that direction. Late winter days in our poorly lit classroom were brightened by drawings of snowdrops done in white and green crayon against a grey paper background. By autumn, yellow-lobed chestnut leaves made their appearance on the table along with shiny brown conkers, and then it was the turn of the yellow and red crayons to be in demand for our seasonal class art display. Everybody's effort was dutifully put up on the wall with large drawing pins but I'd rather that my artistic endeavours had been consigned to the flames in the classroom stove as I never could get the hang of drawing things in any kind of recognisable form.

To her credit, the teacher recognised where my interests lay, however, and was keen to offer encouragement in directions other than drawing. She had a kindly manner when it came to talking about things on the nature table whenever I paused to look at something after the bell rang at the close of the day. As class was packing up one blustery March afternoon, she asked if

I'd seen the rookery in some big trees hidden away up a lane near the school. As soon as we were let out, I went hotfoot along for a look. I stood at the foot of the tall trees, engrossed in the sight of all the black silhouettes wheeling and cawing overhead while their mates sat tight on their eggs in the swaying nests high among the bare branches. Some were arguing and bickering over disputed space while others went in for a bit of surreptitious stick stealing when their neighbour's backs were turned. I hadn't paid much attention to rooks before and I'm not sure I was even familiar with the name. If I'd asked the name of any black *corvid* at home, granny would just have said "Ach, it's jist a craa." To this day, when I look up at all the raucous cawing, stick pinching and general frenetic activity of a spring rookery, I'm still sometimes reminded of that first close encounter with the rookery beside the school.

Summer term came to a close with the prize-giving when endeavour of one type or another was recognised. It was exciting to go up and receive a prize and accompanying limp handshake from the headmistress. My first ever prize was for perfect attendance, an achievement that had been dutifully recorded in fountain pen each day in the meticulously maintained column of blue ticks in the teacher's class register. She took an inordinate pride in keeping a tidy register and delighted in fitting each tick with precision inside the outline of each little red printed square. We could hear her mutter "Oh bother!" if a tick was misplaced and threatened to spoil the look of the whole page.

My first perfect attendance prize was reward for all the trudging back and fore in fine weather and foul for a whole year without missing a single day. The slim volume was full of coloured pictures of penguins in snow-bound Antarctica. It was my first bird book and I couldn't wait to get home to study the artist's illustrations of the smart looking creatures, waddling upright across featureless polar ice floes. In the weeks and months that followed I passed many a wet hour at home poring over the pictures and imagining what life must be like for the birds in their bleak world in the southern wastes. I still have it. Its worn spine says something about the number of times it was opened, though the clean pages are an indication of how carefully it must have been handled. My teacher had obviously had a hand in the choice of subject and she couldn't have made a better one for a child showing an interest in the natural world. I've cause to be grateful because it helped me progress further along the path to a passion that would enrich future travels, with all manner of encounters with wildlife - including penguins in the far south.

*****

The ability to spell properly featured strongly in priorities for learning, with the result that weekly spelling tests were big on the classroom agenda. Some of us managed quite well while others struggled to remember if there was one letter *t* in a word or a double *m* in another. A word that sometimes cropped up in spelling tests as we progressed was 'accommodation'. The teacher never seemed to twig that if you were sitting near one wall you couldn't fail to get it right because it was printed on a large card that had been placed there by officialdom, indicating that 'This classroom provides accommodation for ..... pupils.' (The space allowed for someone to insert the specified number, in this case in the 50s , enough to make a twenty first century teacher go weak at the knees).

Our indoctrination in world geography also came in regular weekly doses. The big coloured political wall map of the world, in keeping with the age in which it had been published, was heavy on the pink shading. We may have been children of the post-war age but the big map reflected the pre-war Empire that had been going strong when the printer's ink was wet. "Pay attention, class!" ordered the teacher as she moved her pointer fondly over the sea of pink that was faraway Canada, India, Australia and New Zealand. "These are the Dominions." We had occasion to be grateful to the Dominions when a former pupil sent a big Christmas box of sweeties over to the school from Canada, though when the teacher read out the letter that came with it, the sender made mention of 'candies.' This was a trifle confusing, because a visitor who came to the house occasionally would bring with her a small white box of home-made Aberdeen candy and the sticky horehound, mint and fruit flavoured pieces didn't look anything like the individually wrapped contents of the Canadian gift parcel. The candy from the Aberdeen shoppie had a tendency to stick to your teeth and refuse to let go. If you weren't careful it could draw them out completely should they happen to be on the loose side.

And so we absorbed the geography of our teacher's pink-tinted world, though that grand world of Empire was already changing, as events in India had already shown. But the old classroom wall map was my first mental reference for the way the Earth was laid out and, strangely enough, I find that somehow it's still in there, like the rookery, lodged in the recesses of my mind.

Chapter 18: Top of the class

Our folks at home would have been none too pleased to know that matters of a personal domestic nature were so freely shared as the three of us made our way to school each day.

"We'd a moose in the hoose last nicht," announced Geordie one morning. "A moose in yer hoose?" I enquired, amused at his unintended poetic twist.

"Aye," Geordie continued, "an ye've nivver seen sic a stramash."

House mice were not unknown visitors at the time but I slowed down to await further enlightenment. "Weel, cam awa wi't," I said, providing him with the opening he was so obviously waiting for.

Geordie took a breath. "Weel," he began, "fan the moose cam oot fae ahin the skirtin boord, wir cattie taen aff across the fleer efter't. Syne the dog taen't intae his noddle tae gyang efter the cat. The dog's tail coupit ma mither's joog o flooers aff the tablie an ma faither drappit his Woodbine doon the front o his semmit." At this point he paused before the denouement of his tale. "Ye should hae seen the sotter." he continued. "The fleer wis sypin weet, ma mither wis neen ower pleased, ma faither got a burnt belly, the cattie wis pitten ootside early, an the dog wis sent awa till his bed.....Fit a tae dee!"

"An fit aboot the moose?" I enquired, out of interest in the rodent's fate.

"Ach, it'll aye be aboot the hoose somewye," replied Geordie. "Like as nae it'll be ettin awa at something in a press – or chawin the tae oot o een o my faither's socks!" I'd a good laugh at that but we all had to quicken our pace as we didn't want to arrive after a teacher had started ringing the brass hand bell.

Things tended to be built on the grand scale in the Victorian age and our classroom was no exception. It had a large floor area, several tall sash windows with thick cords at either side and a high white ceiling into whose cobweb-filled corners no cleaner ever ventured. It had been designed with very large classes in mind and, like the anatomy dissecting theatres of old, ascended in a few steps towards the back, giving everyone a good view of the teacher and her wooden blackboard and easel. In centre stage, our mentor took the place of the cadaver, controlling proceedings from her desk, dressed in customary floral smock. Her tightly permed grey hair was held firmly in place inside a no-nonsense hair net whose edge appeared along her forehead as a thin dark line. She wore stockings with prominent seams up the back and a pair of lacing brown leather shoes that owed more to function than fashion. When the weather was cold and she leaned over to put a shovelful of coal into the heating stove, we sometimes caught a glimpse of the lower edge of her ample pink underwear. If somebody whispered "Tak a look at the teacher's bloomers!" a wave of giggling from both boys and girls spread quickly along the rows.

Like evenly hyowed neeps in a park, we sat in our rows at wooden desks decorated with cast iron ends. Each place was furnished with a small round hole on the right hand side in which reposed a white porcelain inkwell. There was evidently an assumption that the occupant of every seat should be right handed; those who weren't were generally persuaded to be otherwise, as if they suffered from some birth defect that would be better corrected in their own best interests. On the red letter day when we were first allowed to use pens with metal nibs, the inkwells were filled with home-made ink which the teacher, like a conjurer, magically produced with the aid of three props: a white enamel jug filled with water, a short stirring stick and a spoonful or two of mysterious black powder that she kept in a tin in her large cupboard.

The system hadn't really changed that much over the years and previous generations schooled there would have had no difficulty in recognising the place. Parent power had yet to be invented. If anything, parents tended simply to reinforce what happened in school. If you got the strap in school for some misdemeanour, you could expect no sympathy at home, the general philosophy being that if you got it you must have deserved it.

The class was run according to a fundamental principle: work well and be rewarded by changing position. To be 'top of the class' meant just that; you occupied number one place up at the very back of the room. It was a bit like an ascent of Mount Everest; the more effort you put in, the higher the altitude you would attain. Those poor souls who didn't make much of their class work were condemned to a life in the lower regions. There was, however, a seasonal benefit to be had by **not** demonstrating too much proficiency in class tests. In winter, it meant that you were positioned much closer to the stove and therefore to the room's sole source of heating, making lack of academic prowess a decided plus point during a cold spell. If you made really bad mistakes in class work, you ran the risk of acquiring the description of 'dunderheid' among your peers. The community set great store by success in school and I used to get fed up with old wifies constantly asking "Are ye a gweed scholar, ma loon?"

Admonitory ruler in hand, the teacher would leave (less frequently in the coldest days of winter) the vicinity of her desk to wander around the room and inspect our work. At close range, a melange of face powder and chalk dust mingled with a whiff of perfume. The big blackboard rested on top of two wooden pegs on its easel. On its slightly shiny surface she wrote up tests in white chalk prior to our entry into the room before turning the board over to conceal the contents. When all was ready she would reverse the board, the test items now revealed in impeccably straight lines and copperplate writing with flowing loops. The result of every wiping with her cleaning cloth was a fresh layer of dust deposited about her person. When she held her hand out to receive your jotter, I noticed that her fingers, which she sometimes used for the purposes of rubbing out on the board, had chalk dust engrained in the prints. Mind you, I always thought it a bit hypocritical that she used her fingers and the side of her hand to wipe off a bit of writing from the board when we'd had such tirades about spitting on our slates and using cuffs to do the same thing. It was a classic case of "Do as I say and not as I do," though I suppose the real difference was that she was too genteel to put a bit of spit into the cleaning process.

Rote learning was the rule of the day. With the aid of the wall map of Scotland, our knowledge of our native heath was regularly consolidated. "Ready, class..." the teacher would pronounce, standing back from the map and raising her wooden pointer. We were now under starter's orders, awaiting the signal that would send us galloping on our way. Suddenly it came: a sharp rap of the pointer against the map's glossy surface. So well schooled were we in this particular exercise that we needed no further instruction. As the pointer banged against every county in turn, we intoned in unison: "Shetland, Orkney, Caithness, Sutherland, Ross and Cromart*eee*..." This was the point at which we paused to draw breath before racing off again through Inverness-shire and all points south. Not one county was missed on our chanted, whistle-stop tour, not even the humblest shires of Kinross and Clackmannan, so small in area that the mapmaker didn't even have room to insert their full names. They had to be content with an ignominious K and C, but at least they were shown in their proper places; the poor souls in Shetland and Orkney had to put up with having their islands enclosed in little boxes in the sea somewhere off Aberdeen.

I recall only a single visit from a school inspector. How a class preformed was naturally a matter of pride to any teacher and we were warned to be on our best behaviour when the expected visitor entered the room. We needed no reminding to stand up when he came in since that was the way of doing things. The house rule was that we stood up smartly every time the headmistress entered and we were not given the all clear to sit down till she had made a thorough job of scanning the class. She had a particular eye for spotting anyone leaning on their desk instead of standing up at the acceptable angle. "**Don't** slouch, boys!" was her favourite rebuke, uttered with a kind of sniff, as though we slouchers were releasing a bad smell. Naturally, our teacher was mortified if such admonition should be given to anyone in her class and you could be sure that the offender would pay for the slouching as soon as the headmistress had left the room. The inspector's visit was all very formal. He was a dapper man with dark suit and neatly trimmed moustache, as befitted someone of his official status, and he carried a small case as a badge of office. From the front of the class he asked some general knowledge questions in a humourless kind of way. Meanwhile, the teacher stood down at her desk, fixing us with her lion-tamer's look, willing that `she wouldn't be mortified by some glaikit individual putting up his or her hand and giving a daft answer. Such things could easily happen, and must have been a real dread during an inspection.

The ultimate reward for classroom excellence was the position of honour up at the back. It was easier to manage the odd bit of chat at the back if you kept your head down and whispered. Down at the front was a strictly no-go zone for talking, where any attempt at blethering was instantly quashed by a withering look. Of course, you could also be demoted to the lower ranks through some minor misdemeanour. "Pack your bag and come down here!" was then the stern command and, if you happened to be the chosen one, you had to endure the shame of gathering your chattels together and heading down with all eyes fixed upon you. This moving up and down according to accomplishment or behaviour smacked a bit of snakes and ladders but, in place of coloured counters, it was real live pupils who made the moves.

Being top of the class definitely had its down side. Not only did you run the risk of being called a teacher's pet but you might have the mark of Cain put upon you in the form of the weekly class medal. The Friday afternoon presentation was more like an investiture, the teacher doing the honours as formally as if she was the monarch at the Palace dishing out gongs. Whoever was deemed to have performed best during the week had to go down to the front of the class and have the class medal pinned to his or her chest. To make matters worse, any errand requiring to be run on the school premises was given as an added reward, reinforcing the 'teacher's pet' side of things.

Modesty does not forbid me from saying that the award of the medal befell me on one or two occasions, though I can only think that they must have been on weeks that weren't too heavy on the mathematical side of things. The medal in question, with its faded red ribbon, had perhaps been awarded for service during the Great War, or even the Boer War before that. In its new role, it was supposed to be worn in and out of school as a mark of achievement. To me, it was a bronze curse pinned to my hand-knitted grey jersey and the sooner it came off the better. The Friday afternoon medal ceremony was just one more echo of the military about the place. Another one was that boys were expected to salute the teacher should you happen to meet her in the street. The girls were similarly meant to recognise her status in the community and show respect in an appropriate lady-like manner by dropping a mild curtsey. Needless to say, if you saw the teacher coming, you swiftly crossed to the other side of the street and made a show of studying whatever was on display in the nearest shop window, even if whatever was in it wasn't of the slightest interest. All these old ways, combined with the fading maps of Empire hanging on the classroom walls, were relics of an age that was rapidly coming to an end.

Chewing in class was like nibbling at forbidden fruit and strictly frowned upon. But that didn't stop us from attempting to insert the odd Buttanut sweetie surreptitiously into our mouths when we thought the teacher was looking elsewhere. These favourites of the time looked like orange pandrops, but whatever was used for the colouring started to fade as soon you started sucking at them. As a result, there was an irresistible tendency to take out a partly sooked sweetie and examine it to see how much of the colour had worn off, though that wasn't always such a good idea, especially if you should happen to drop it on to the floor. If the teacher saw or heard it fall, you would instantly incur her displeasure, and even if she didn't witness what happened, the thing would be so covered in floor fluff and dust that a perfectly good sweetie would have gone to waste.

We couldn't have been short of physical exercise with the long walk back and fore to school but, even so, we had to bring our black canvas sandshoes to school each week and dutifully exercise our limbs in drill, whose very name was another hint of the military. Following the example of our drill instructor, we all threw our arms and legs out and in, and bean bags to one another (more often **at** one another when the instructor's back was turned). We also endeavoured to get thin wooden hoops to revolve at speed around our bellies. It was all pretty tame stuff but there was a bit of more serious competition once a year in the sports. As much as anything the sports afternoon was a welcome escape from the stuffy confines of the classroom, an occasion where you needed to apply a bit of native cunning if you were to get anywhere. In our sweaty footwear we ran the three-legged race with one leg tied to that of a partner. In the wheelbarrow race, the trick was to avoid going forward too fast over the grass on the palms of your hands if you were the 'barrow', as it was easy to lose balance and collapse to one side. The key to success in the tattie and spoon race was to find a tattie that was suited by nature to sitting in a spoon if you wanted it to stay in place when you made a dash for the finishing line. If it was a big, old and unevenly shaped Kerr's Pink that was starting to sprout, you were doomed from the start as the chances were that it would tumble off long before you reached the sawdust finishing line. The sack race was never my event till I realised that if you got in quick and rummaged for the widest possible hessian bag, you also had the key to success. With a bigger sack, you could put one foot into each corner, hold the top round about your waist and run instead of having to jump – not exactly in the Olympic spirit, perhaps, but the narrower sacks made you fall over, whereas the wider ones allowed more freedom with your legs.

I went past my old school a few years ago. I couldn't get over how much it had shrunk from the impressive structure that had been locked away in my memory all those years. Of course, it was all to do with the way you view things when you're little but the playground really had diminished, giving way to a range of new buildings. The open-fronted shelter shed where we crowded together to protect ourselves from the elements, like a herd of nowt taking cover from a storm, had vanished and with it the granite-walled ootside lavvies. *Sic transit gloria mundi!*

Chapter 19: Winter woes

When it comes to winter weather, everybody seems to remember the worst times. Winters somehow seemed far colder and snow drifts much higher in days gone by. But the combination of short legs and deep snow fairly slowed down our progress to school on coorse wintry days, and things weren't helped by a constant urge to get up to devilment by throwing sna bas, or trying to creep up behind to stuff snow down one another's necks. A handful of cold, wet snow thrust down a sark collar must definitely rank as one of life's less pleasant sensations. Naturally, this then required retaliation and that wasted even more time.

When the overnight temperature plunged low enough to make unprotected ears nip, some old mannie we'd encounter on the way, out for his Press & Journal to start his day with a scan through the death notices or for his nicotine fix of Bogie Roll, was bound to say something like "Aye loons, ye've the richt thing on yer heids the day. That frost's aneugh tae tak the lugs aff ye." The reference was to our standard winter headgear of woollen knitted balaclava in assorted colours, or brown leather helmet, both of which were our defences against possible ear drop in extreme cold. The latter was modelled on a military flying helmet and yet another echo of the age in which we lived. Like Biggles setting out on a mission, we trudged our way to school, helmet secured under the chin with a thin strap and small buckle. All the larking about without proper reference to time (none of the three of us possessed a watch) naturally increased the danger of arriving late for school and risking a teacher's displeasure. As we well knew, come rain or shine, hell or high water, the teachers were sticklers for time keeping and gave no quarter to latecomers, except in the most extreme conditions. They clearly regarded it as one of their missions in life to instil the virtues of punctuality into their charges and they responded to that calling with missionary zeal.

Half way to school our route took us past a granite horse troch that still sat by the roadside, having witnessed the transition from horse cart to motor lorry in the matter of conveying goods. In its heyday it would have been a boon to working horses going about their duties, pulling heavy loads along the road. Those days had all but gone but the troch was still in working order and we sometimes stopped to take a drink on a warm summer's afternoon where cart horses once slaked their thirst, putting our mouths under the trickle of cool water that flowed into one side of the long granite basin. In really cold winter weather the surface froze over and we never missed an opportunity to break the ice with a stone and try to lift out the slippery thick slabs. What the horses used to do when the troch froze over I'm not sure. Maybe, like us, they didn't fancy a drink of icy water on the cold days anyway. On really frosty mornings, we were always keen to take a detour round by the burn to marvel at the long, pointed icicles hanging from part of an old water wheel and to see the frozen splashes that had built up on the tall dead waterside grasses before they yielded to the extra weight and bent right over.

The edifice in which the education authority prepared us for the life to come looked even less welcoming as we approached it on a dark midwinter morning. A dour looking place at the best of times, any dreich day seemed to put the school's grey granite stonework into even darker humour. But in really cold weather there was one great saving grace: the coal-burning stove that stood down at the front. Its positioning was quite fortuitous, since the teacher was never so inclined to move so far away on a chilly winter's morning, preferring to conduct her lessons with her back to the stove so as to derive the full benefit of the radiating warmth on her nether regions.

There was one serious seasonal drawback to the school, however. It had been built when the creature comforts of the young weren't too high on the list of priorities of the authority. People talk about the character building value of cold showers in private schools, but in my opinion we had something far more testing. In the matter of going out to answer any call of nature in winter, austerity ruled. When louring, snow-laden clouds filled the sky and outsize flakes of snow drifted down past the high classroom windows, we'd have done anything but put a hand up and ask out of class should nature call, so we just crossed our legs and tried not to think about it till bell time. When the snow was "fair dingin doon," as they said, it was only when need was at its most pressing that anyone was brave enough to venture out into the icy wastes. The reason for the reluctance was simple: the matching stone-built conveniences sat in splendid isolation some distance from the main building. In the warmer days of summer, this was something of an olfactory blessing. These ootside lavvies were the very antithesis of comfort, being open to the sky and receiving the uninterrupted benefit of all the precipitation that the heavens cared to shower down upon them. As a result, the ground surface inside was frequently wet and if the overnight frost had been severe, the place was transformed into a skating rink. All this wouldn't have been so bad had it not been for the fact that the loons' facilities consisted in the main of a long and shallow, cement-lined depression that sloped down gradually at one end towards an outlet. In the warmer summer days the place was much frequented by flies. Following a good overnight fall of snow, an opportunity arose for the first boy out to the Spartan facilities in the morning to indulge in some creative artwork on a pristine white canvas.

We were never slow to exploit any opportunities for fun at the quines' expense and snowy winter days were heaven sent for the purpose. After one especially big fall the scene was set for an incident that is writ large in my memory. As we were being herded out at into the snow at playtime to amuse ourselves as best we could, we received the customary dire warning about snowballs and possible broken windows. "This school's not made of money!" was one of our teacher's favourite mantras, displaying a frugality that must have gone down well in the austere war years. Of course, the basic outside conveniences had not a pane of glass about them, getting all the light anybody might need from the heavens above.

This particular heavy snowfall offered too good an opportunity to miss, and some of us took it into our heads to have (as we thought) a harmless bit of fun in lobbing snowballs, in the manner of hand grenades, over the high wall into the quines' quarters. For a few minutes, we maintained a steady barrage, obviously giving the occupants plenty of entertainment, to judge by all the giggling and skirls. Had we stuck with these modestly shaped missiles, things might not have gone the way they did, but the snowballs got bigger and the skirling got louder, leading to the sudden appearance of one of the teachers. Clad in her winter wardrobe of galoshes, heavy dark woollen coat and hastily applied red head square knotted under her chin, she was neither the last word in elegance nor looked too pleased at being dragged out of a nice warm staff room to deal with the commotion outside. One of the quines decided to clype immediately, notwithstanding the fact that she'd been enjoying the whole thing as much as any of them. The result was that the six of us were summarily marched off.

Once inside, we were ordered to line up in silence in the corridor outside the scary varnished brown door to await the headmistress's pleasure. By this time our hands were so red that

150

they fairly dirled when we came into the warmth and I was beginning to wonder what the added impact of a bit of leather might be. Lobbing outsize sna bas in this manner would definitely constitute an offence serious enough to be punishable by a dose of the strap, the time-honoured instrument of corporal punishment that was taken out and exercised from time to time on miscreants' palms. The longer the headmistress was in coming, the more time we had to contemplate our fate. The trouble was that she was taking such a long time to appear that we knew fine we'd now be in double trouble as we'd be arriving late back to our class. I realise now that she was probably observing the customary wait devised by teachers as a mild form of mental torture, letting you stew for a while and giving you time to imagine a worse and worse punishment the longer you had to think about it.

When, at last, the commandant arrived we were given a look as frosty as the ground outside and ushered brusquely into her room. She shut the door with a deliberately loud bang and we all jumped. In appearance, she wasn't that robust looking a woman but the green tweed costume gave her a severe look that was reinforced by the round-rimmed spectacles perched on her nose. As she fixed each one of us in turn with her scariest glare I could feel a shiver run down my spine. We were treated to what seemed like a five minute homily on how ashamed we should be and how she would have no option but to deal with the matter in the severest possible way.

My eye drifted over to her desk in search of the dreaded strap but there was none to be seen. Instead, she had decided on her own form of punishment for dealing with annoyances of this nature. After the first lamb to the slaughter, she moved slowly along the line, lifting each body nearly off the ground as she applied a shaking with a strength that belied her physical form. I knew then what a rat must feel like when a terrier gets hold of it.

We'd none of us encountered anything like it, but all I can say is that such vigorous shaking with intent to frighten was mightily effective. What the consequences of such a well-shoogled brain might have been for me in later life I'm probably not the one to judge. By the time she'd finished with the sixth in line she was fairly getting into the swing of things and looked as if she might be fit to tackle another half dozen more. At last, after a final harangue, we were free to go; back to whatever further censure awaited us when we knocked apprehensively on our classroom door. The pair of clypie cloots steered well clear of us for the rest of the week, never so much as looking in our direction for fear of having their pigtails pulled after school.

Forbidden pleasures are always the best and that was definitely the case with the playground slides which we made in snowy weather out of sight of the staffroom window. After a good run at a slide, there was a brief moment of exhilaration as you propelled yourself across the glassy surface. Being shod in a pair of tackety boots on a long, icy slide was like having on a pair of racing skates, much enhancing the sensation of speed. The teachers generally turned a bit of a blind eye when a slide was made, knowing full well that by next morning the joys of propulsion over the ice would be but a memory after the janitor had applied his customary shovelful of warm cinders and put an end to the fun. Next morning, we would look sadly upon the jannie's scattered ashes on the sabotaged slide and contemplate where we might start a fresh one.

The classroom stove came into its own on winter days. Not only did it radiate warmth, but soaking wet clothes could be arranged around the wire guard to get some heat. In terms of disagreeability, the smell of steaming gabardine coat was by far the worst. By the afternoon, clothes were dry and ready to get wet all over again on our way home. The stove was decidedly multifunctional. During particularly bad spells of weather, a difficulty arose with the supplies delivered each morning from the dairy a few miles out in the country. The brown and white Ayrshire cows obligingly supplied the milk to fill the small glass bottles (one third of a pint) that were issued free each day as the Government's contribution to growing healthy bodies for the nation's future good. The top of each bottle was closed with a circular cardboard top which, in turn, had a small bit that could be pushed in with a drinking straw. This was the only permitted method of consumption and the teacher was on constant milk time alert to spot any of the loons bold enough to remove the top and drink straight out of the bottle. A weather related problem arose after the milk had been sitting for an hour or two on the exposed back of the lorry on a freezing cold morning. According to a basic law of physics, milk freezes and expands and the obvious way to go in a bottle is upwards. Naturally, this forced the tops right up. In those days the milk contained a good proportion of cream and the result was that each bottle developed a circular protrusion of frozen yellow milk, with the pushed-up cardboard top sitting above like a little hat.

Generally speaking, the teacher made sure that the metal milk crate was positioned beside the stove to thaw out the contents, but we never forgot the morning she set a few bottles above the quiescent stove, thinking that she would speed up the process. Unfortunately, the result was not as intended. With a sudden hiss of steam, at first one bottle split, then another, followed by a disagreeable smell of singeing milk that permeated the room for hours afterwards and forced her to grab hold of the ropes on either side of the big windows and let them down to allow a stream of Arctic air to whistle round our bare knees. The unpleasantness of this experience, however, paled into insignificance compared to the taste taken on by the milk when the cows were housed indoors in the byre and fed a surfeit of neeps. The resulting neepy taste rendered the milk really unpalatable and there was also the occasional unpleasant smell as somebody nearby riftit with their mouth open, provoking a muttered chorus of complaint from those in the immediate vicinity. The teacher didn't help any by insisting that we drink up every last drop, no matter how tainted. "Milk is good for growing strong bones" she opined, but I bet **she'd** never been forced to down a bottle of the neep-flavoured variety.

*****

And so the seasons came and went: winter changing to spring and spring in its turn into summer in the satisfying rhythm that had run through the eight decades of my granny's life and the first of mine. The lengthening spring days would once more turn the puddocks' fancy to what puddocks fancy doing at that season of the year, but there would be no more forays with bandy net and jam jar to the amphibians' time honoured spawning place. At the age of ten, I said a last goodbye to my granny as she was laid to rest among her ain folk in the quiet old kirkyard.

Circumstances now determined that I take up the threads of a new life, this time among fisher folk whose coastal spik was different in intonation, pronunciation and even in vocabulary. First impressions were of a bleaker, windswept place; the one which the seagulls forsook for the shelter of the inland howe when winter storms unleashed their fury on the cliffs and flung sea spume high into the air. But this new setting brought new opportunities: lying on a carpet of sea pinks on a summer cliff-top, peering at clown-faced puffins at their nesting burrows down below; watching whiter than white gannets on long summer evenings as they plummeted into the sea like a rain of darts; marvelling at the aerobatic skills of piratical skuas as they harried the terns on blustery autumn days. Such things became my new markers in the seasons' round.

In the course of time I found myself sitting in a lecture room in the ancient precincts of King's College in Old Aberdeen, beneath the chapel's sandstone crown. It was a summer's day and the afternoon air was still and sultry. In the academic atmosphere of the place, with its smell of old varnished wood and gently baking dust, my mind wandered off when it should rightly have been concentrated on the Professor of English as he stood, black-gowned, delivering his sage words from a lectern down at the front. The words rose up, just as our teacher's had done from her station beside the stove in winter days, when the smell of neepy milk pervaded the classroom air. As I idly contemplated how the old wooden bench seats around me had been polished by a succession of student posteriors, my mind irreverently drifted back to those happy days up among the high stuey seats on mart days. Half listening to my mentor's intoned words as he quoted the poet Wordsworth, my ears suddenly became fixed on one line: *"Bliss was it in that dawn to be alive, but to be young was very heaven!"*

Now, it's highly questionable that the Lake District romantic would ever have had the chance to chase a wayward stirk through the heart of his nearest market town, and I'd certainly bet Wordsworth's granny never entertained an elephant in her lobby. But the poet's words took on a special meaning at that moment, as my mind drifted back to past times. Heaven-sent they certainly seemed, those blissful years of my early growing in the broad green howe.